Jung's Evolving Views of Nazi Germany:

From the Nazi Takeover to the End of World War II

William Schoenl and Linda Schoenl

CHIRON PUBLICATIONS • ASHEVILLE, NORTH CAROLINA

www.ChironPublicatons.com

Interior and cover design by Danijela Mijailović
Printed primarily in the United States of America.

ISBN 978-1-63051-407-5 paperback
ISBN 978-1-63051-408-2 hardcover
ISBN 978-1-63051-409-9 electronic

Library of Congress Cataloging-in-Publication Data

Names: Schoenl, William J., 1941- author.
Title: Jung's evolving views of Nazi Germany : from the Nazi takeover
    to the end of World War II / William Schoenl and Linda Schoenl.
Description: Asheville, North Carolina : Chiron Publications, 2016. |
    Includes bibliographical references and index.
Identifiers: LCCN 2016044644 (print) | LCCN 2016046110 (ebook) |
    ISBN 9781630514082 (hbk : alk. paper) | ISBN 9781630514075 (pbk
    : alk. paper) | ISBN 9781630514099 (e-book)
Subjects: LCSH: Jung, C. G. (Carl Gustav), 1875-1961. | Jungian psy-
    chology. | National socialism--Germany. | Germany--Politics and
    government--1933-1945.
Classification: LCC BF109.J86 S36 2016 (print) | LCC BF109.J86 (ebook)
    | DDC 150.19/54092--dc23
LC record available at https://lccn.loc.gov/2016044644

Cover photo Anschluss sudetendeutscher Gebiete: Bundesarchiv, Bild
146-1970-005-28 / CC-BY-SA 3.0

Contents

Preface

This book examines for the first time Jung's views of Nazi Germany during the entire period from the Nazi takeover in 1933 until the end of World War II. It brings together our research in archives and primary sources over the past ten years.

Chapter 1 sets forth reasons for Jung's actions in Nazi Germany's first year. It brings forth evidence that, besides wanting to preserve psychotherapy in Germany and maintain the international connection between German and other psychotherapists, he wanted to advance Jungian psychology—his psychology—in Germany. It also presents evidence that acknowledges he occasionally made some anti-Semitic statements during this early period but that he was not anti-Semitic as Nazis were. Next it demonstrates that after Gustav Bally's criticisms in the *Neue Zuercher Zeitung* in February 1934, Jung entered into a transition in spring 1934 during which he became warier of the Nazis and of statements that might seem anti-Semitic. The chapter shows very significant changes in Jung's views both of the Nazis and of anti-Semitic statements during the important early period from January 1933—when Hitler became Chancellor of Germany—through the spring of 1934.

Chapter 2 shows that after spring 1934, it is untenable to hold that Jung was a "Nazi sympathizer." He became still warier of the Nazis from 1934 to 1936. By March 1936, his attitude toward the

Nazis had taken a further turn: it was clearly more pessimistic than a year earlier. The chapter next shows Jung's evolving views of Nazi Germany from 1936 to the beginning of World War II. In an October 1936 lecture at the Tavistock Clinic, London, he made his strongest and most negative statements to date about Nazi Germany. While in Berlin in September 1937 for lectures to the Jung *Gesellschaft*, his observations of Hitler at a military parade led him to conclude that, should the catastrophe of war come, it would be far more and bloodier than he had previously supposed. In interviews after the Sudetenland Crisis in the fall of 1938, Jung made stronger comments on Hitler and Nazi Germany. When Hitler invaded Poland in September 1939, Jung said that the conviction existed in Switzerland that Germany had lost its national honor to an unspeakable degree.

Chapter 3 shows how strongly anti-Nazi Jung's views were in relation to such events during World War II as the fall of France, the bombings of Britain, the U.S. entry into the War, and Allied troops advancing into Germany. It also shows the beginnings and development of allegations in the United States in 1944 that Jung was pro-Nazi. Esther Harding and Eleanor Bertine, two prominent Jungian psychologists in New York City, kept Jung informed of the allegations. This chapter is based on manuscripts in the Jung Archives in Zurich, the FBI reports on Jung, and other primary sources. It demonstrates Jung's evolving views from 1939 to the war's end in 1945.

The Epilogue, Chapter 4, discusses the post-war attacks on Jung in 1945-46. S.S. Feldman's article, "Dr. C.G. Jung and National Socialism," appeared in the *American Journal of Psychiatry*—official organ of the American Psychiatric Association—in September

Preface

1945. In a letter to the *New York Herald Tribune*, one of the largest newspapers in the United States, Albert D. Parelhoff supported Feldman's article and charged that Jung had been pro-Nazi in his views and actions. Bertine and Harding responded in a letter to the *Tribune*, and Gotthard Booth, Gerhard Adler, and Ernest Harms defended Jung in letters to the *American Journal of Psychiatry*. Their defenses of Jung, however, had a significant weakness: they did not recognize that his views of the Nazis changed after Nazi Germany's first year and that his views of Nazi Germany evolved during the following years. Parelhoff became Jung's most persistent attacker and, in a series of articles in *The Protestant* beginning in June-July 1946, falsely alleged that Jung was a Nazi collaborator.

Our interactions with many scholars during our years of research and writing have been a particular pleasure. We express special thanks to Deirdre Bair, Murray Stein, Ann Conrad Lammers, and Giovanni Sorge. We are grateful to the archivists of the Jung Archives, Swiss Federal Institute of Technology, Zurich; C.G. Jung Biographical Archive, Harvard Countway Library of Medicine, Boston; C.G. Jung Foundation for Analytical Psychology archives, New York; Virginia Allan Detloff Library and archives, C.G. Jung Institute of San Francisco; and the Joseph and Jane Hollister Wheelwright Collection, Opus Archives, Pacifica Graduate Institute, Santa Barbara. We are thankful to Richard R. Laurence for translations of unpublished letters from the German. We alone are responsible for any errors in this book.

William Schoenl and Linda Schoenl

Acknowledgments

We gratefully acknowledge: the appearance of parts of Chapter 1 in Schoenl & Schoenl (2016), "Jung's Views of Nazi Germany: The First Year and Jung's Transition," *Journal of Analytical Psychology, 61(4), 481-96 (Society of Analytical Psychology and Blackwell Publishing)*; of Chapters 1 and 2 in Schoenl & Peck (2012), "An Answer to the Question: Was Jung, for a Time, a 'Nazi Sympathizer' or Not?," *Jung Journal: Culture & Psyche*, 6(4), 98-105 (C. G. Jung Institute of San Francisco and the University of California Press); of Chapters 2 and 3 in Schoenl (2014), "Jung's Evolving Views of Nazi Germany: From 1936 to the End of World War II," *Journal of Analytical Psychology*, 59(2), 245-62 (Society of Analytical Psychology and Blackwell Publishing); of Chapters 3 and 4 in Schoenl (2009), "The World War II Attacks on Jung: Eleanor Bertine's and Esther Harding's Perspectives," *Quadrant*, 39(1), 17-27 (C.G. Jung Foundation for Analytical Psychology).

Chapter 1
Nazi Germany's First Year and Jung's Transition: 1933-Spring 1934

Jung's views during Nazi Germany's first year

Three months after Hitler became Chancellor of Germany in January 1933, Joseph Henderson, who was studying medicine in London to prepare for a career as an analytical psychologist, wrote to Jung asking his reaction to the Hitler regime. To Henderson, it sometimes seemed, on the one hand, like a positive phase of the German people's coming to consciousness and, on the other hand, like a hopelessly regressive movement (Henderson 1933). Jung responded that he did not know about the Nazi movement: it might bring some new thing of value into the world or it might just carry off people to their madness (Henderson 1968, 16). A theme of N.A. Lewin's book, *Jung on War, Politics and Nazi Germany: Exploring the Theory of Archetypes and the Collective Unconscious* (2009), is that Jung saw Nazi Germany in the 1930s in archetypal terms. We agree with this view.

An entry in the unpublished "Notebooks" of Esther Harding, a prominent Jungian psychologist in New York, corroborates this point regarding Jung's ambivalence towards the Nazi movement in 1933. She recorded that in an analytic hour with him in

Kuesnacht on November 6, he said that old Wotan, the wind god [an archetype], had begun to blow in Germany and nobody knew what would happen. Some officials in Germany had told him that they neither knew the meaning of what was happening nor where it was tending, but it was their experiment. It might lead to chaos or hell, but it was their experiment. Jung said that was his own attitude—this was their own experiment (Harding 1933, p. 358). An unpublished BBC radio interview with Aniela Jaffe (1975) further corroborates this point regarding Jung in 1933 not knowing where the Nazi movement was tending: she said one should admit that Jung made mistakes and that at a certain time he gave the Nazi movement a chance. She added that he was not the only person to give it a chance at the time (Jaffe 1975, 23).

Jung accepted the presidency of the General Medical Society for Psychotherapy (hereafter abbreviated GMSP) in 1933 after Ernst Kretschmer resigned as president in April. Lammers (2012a) pointed out that Jung accepted its presidency on condition that the Society would be restructured as an international organization, politically neutral. He "never worked in a nazified organization." On the contrary, in 1933 he saw an international GMSP as "a way to stay connected with the German community of psycho-therapists and protect the future of psychotherapy in Germany, without succumbing to the policies of the Reich" (pp. 99, 106). Lammers (2012a) further observed that a motive of Jung in becoming president of the GMSP may have been to promote his psychology in Germany: "His school of analytical psychology stood to be promoted in Germany, while Freud's was systematically suppressed. He cannot have failed to realize that this shift in the balance of power between his school and Freud's gave him and his followers an advantage" (p. 106). We recognize the foregoing facts and viewpoints, and we do not see them as contradicting the research that we bring forth in this chapter. Schoenl and Peck (2012) showed that Jung's views of Nazi Germany changed from 1933 to March 1936. The present chapter demonstrates significant changes in Jung's views both of the Nazis and of anti-Semitic statements from 1933 through Jung's transition in spring 1934.

In June 1933, Jung officially became president of the General Medical Society for Psychotherapy. Jung said he accepted the presidency to support the profession of psychotherapy which seemed gravely threatened in Germany and to preserve the international connection between psychotherapists in Germany and those elsewhere (Jung 1935a; Jung 1973, p. 135, Jung to Swedish psychotherapist Poul Bjerre, 22 January 1934). In addition to these two reasons, we believe that Jung acted as he did for a third reason: to advance Jungian psychology—his psychology—in Germany. To begin with an example, he wrote to Christian Jenssen in Cologne on 29 May 1933 that, while in the Anglo-Saxon world he had been known for a long time, unfortunately in Germany he was not well-known (Jung 1973, p. 122). Sherry (2010) identifies Christian Jenssen as the pseudonym of Gottfried Martin, an editor and art critic in Cologne (p. 108). On 28 March 1934, Jung wrote to Max Guggenheim, a colleague in Lausanne, that Freud once rightly told him that the fate of psychotherapy would be decided in Germany (Jung 1973, p. 156).

On 9 June 1933, Jung told J. H. Schultz, a German neurologist, that Walter Cimbal, secretary-general of the GMSP and a German psychotherapist, had informed Jung that the GMSP was not being dissolved (Jung 1973, p. 124). In view of the fact that psychotherapists in the GMSP's German section would have to coordinate with the Nazi German regime (*Gleichschaltung*)—otherwise the section would not survive—Jung wrote Cimbal on 4 September 1933 that they accepted the existing political conditions as actuality. Jung remarked that one could not say about any political movement that it was right or wrong, and psychotherapy must be able to cope with external realities. They could fulfill their scientific task in this context (Jung 1933a). In Jung's view, given the political situation, this was pragmatic.

In an entry in her unpublished notebooks, Esther Harding recorded some statements by Jung that have hitherto been un-published and that seem in some degree anti-Semitic. In her analytic hour with him on 6 November 1933 in Kuesnacht, she recorded that he said East met West in eastern Germany and strange things happened in this balance-wheel and that Jews always congregated by such a balance point, for they fish in troubled waters. She wrote that he said he was sorry for individual hardship, but he felt that the Jews as a whole had deserved it. German Jews had congregated at Montreaux, Switzerland, when Germany was starving, and drank champagne. He further said that relatively few Jews had been expelled, Jewish shops in Berlin went on the same, and anti-Semitic feeling occurred only in places like Germany or New York (Harding 1933, p. 358). Jung may have gotten these views from the contemporary culture where he lived. We agree with Aryeh Maidenbaum who, in the conclusion of his book *Jung and the Shadow of Anti-Semitism* (2002/2003), wrote that Jung "did undergo change in the course of his life" and that "in private, it appears that Jung did come to understand his own shadow issues surrounding the so-called 'Jewish question.' Having

4

spoken to many of his students, analysands, and others in Jung's inner circle, it seems to me that any anti-Semitism that can be attributed to Jung (and in his early career there clearly exists enough of his writings to make such a case) should be attributed to a cultural, unconscious prejudice on his part and not what one would define as consciously anti-Semitic" (Maidenbaum 2002/2003, p. 217).

Jung was at no time anti-Semitic as Nazis were. His letter to Rudolf Allers, a Jewish Austrian psychotherapist and follower of Alfred Adler, 23 November 1933—the same month as his comments to Harding—illustrates this point. In spite of Nazi anti-Semitism Jung asked Allers to continue as editor of the reviews section of the *Zentralblatt fuer Psychotherapie*, the GMSP's journal. As president of the Society Jung was its editor. Jung told Allers that Professor Matthias H. Goering, now director of the German section of the GMSP, was a very amiable and reasonable man and that Jung had best hopes for their cooperation (Jung 1973, pp. 131-32). In 1933 Jung was less wary both of the Nazis and of anti-Semitic statements than he later became. His views of them and Matthias Goering would change in 1934.

In December 1933, Jung published a somewhat ambiguously worded editorial in the *Zentralblatt fuer Psychotherapie*. He may have worded it ambiguously with one eye to Nazi readers and the other eye to his own meaning. He wrote that, due to Kretschmer's resignation, he had become president of the Society and Editor of the *Zentralblatt* and this "change coincided with the great political upheaval in Germany." He went on to say that although psychotherapy as a science had nothing to do with politics, a confusion of views and doctrines not unlike the prior state of affairs in politics currently marked the state of affairs in psychotherapy. The primary task of the *Zentralblatt*, therefore, would be impartially to appreciate all objective contributions and promote an overall view that would do more justice to the basic facts of the human psyche. Then, in a statement that became controversial, he wrote that the "differences which actually do exist between Germanic and Jewish psychology and which have long been known to every intelligent person are no longer to be glossed over, and this can only be beneficial to science." But he added, in a statement omitted by some future critics, that he "should like to state expressly that this implies no depreciation of Semitic psychology, any more than it is a depreciation of the Chinese to speak of the peculiar psychology of the Oriental" (Jung 1933b, paras. 1014-15). Lammers (2012a) has noted that the "German language became contaminated— Joerg Rasche's term—by Nazi jargon (Rasche 2007, p. 19). The writings of the era, even passages written by enemies and victims of Hitler's regime, are startling in how often they contain words and phrases from the Nazi lexicon. Pollution of the German language by Nazi jargon sometimes makes it difficult to fix the nature and degree of anti-Semitism in Jung's writings of the early 1930s" (Lammers 2012a, p. 112). Rasche (2012) noted that "many formulations used by Jung or his disciples in 1933 and 1934, or even by [Martin] Buber [the famous Jewish existential philosopher], make strange reading today. Some words have become contaminated…. Even when contemplating Jung's statements about 'Jewish psychology' in 1933, I find it important to bear in mind the ways this theme was discussed in general terms for decades, even in psychoanalytic circles…. He [Jung] intended no devaluing of 'Jewish psychology' as he already stated in his 'Editorial' and testified again, over and over" (pp. 68-69).

In the same issue of the *Zentralblatt*, a statement by Matthias Goering appeared in which he committed the members of the GMSP's German section to reading Hitler's *Mein Kampf* thoroughly and conscientiously. Although Jung had thought Goering's statement would appear only in a special German issue, had not approved its appearance in the *Zentralblatt*, and subsequently expressed to colleagues his displeasure that it had appeared there (Jung 1973, pp. 144-47, 149-51), its appearance also provided fuel for contemporary and future critics.

Besides Jung's editorial in the *Zentralblatt*, his letters in December 1933 to Wolfgang Kranefeldt, a German colleague formerly in Zurich and now a practicing psychotherapist in Berlin, and Gustav Richard Heyer, an analytical psychologist in Germany, and a further letter in February 1934 to Kranefeldt all indicate Jung wanted to advance Jungian psychology in Germany in place of Freud's psychology. On 20 December 1933, he wrote Kranefeldt that the *Zentralblatt* would like an article from Kranefeldt on Jewish and Aryan psychology, especially a critical investigation and evaluation of Freud's *Civilization and Its Discontents*. He should also include Freud's *Ego and the Id* and *The Future of an Illusion*, for Freud put forth the clearest statement of his "negative" Jewish standpoint in these works. In contrast, Kranefeldt should highlight and support Jung's standpoint with exact quotations. Thus, readers could be informed about the essential issues by comparing Freud's basic principles and philosophical convictions with Jung's. Kranefeldt would not find this task difficult since he was thoroughly versed in this aspect (Jung 1933c). On 20 December 1933, Jung also wrote to Heyer that the *Zentralblatt* would like an article from him on the development of ideas from Freud's sexual psychology to Jung's standpoint. He told Heyer that it was extremely important at the present moment for the prevailing confusion of ideas in the field of psychotherapy to be clarified. Among doctors, there were too many who lacked the time, desire, or money to study the literature themselves. They formed their opinions mainly from short articles (Jung 1933d).

On 9 February 1934 Jung wrote Kranefeldt that "the Aryan people can point out that with Freud and Adler specifically Jewish points of view are publicly preached, and as can be proven likewise, points of view that have an essentially corrosive character. If the proclamation of this Jewish gospel is agreeable to the government, then so be it. Otherwise there is also the possibility that this would not be agreeable to the government" (Jung 1934a). This letter was not made available to us in the Jung Archives, Zurich. The letter indicates that Jung favored some suppression by the German government of public preaching of Freudian psychology. In the concluding chapter to his book, Maidenbaum (2002/2003) observed: "Notwithstanding Jung's explanation that he was accepting the presidency [of the GMSP] for the purpose of helping from within, there is little doubt that advancing his own theories was an important factor for him." After interviewing C.A. Meier, Jung's colleague in Zurich who became Secretary of the international GMSP in 1934, Maidenbaum concluded: "In short, Meier validated my own thoughts that, notwithstanding the fact that consciously Jung believed he was helping his Jewish colleagues, the shadow of power and recognition in the field were in all likelihood motivations that had to be taken into account. His [Meier's] admission, difficult to extract, left no doubt: 'Yes, correct, I mean as much as it was devaluating Freud, they might value Jung so much more, you know? That came into it no doubt'" (pp. 202-203). Jung's unpublished letters to Kranefeldt and Heyer of 20 December 1933 and his letter to Kranefeldt of 9 February 1934 that we have presented above provide further evidence that a factor for Jung was advancing his psychology.

In his article, "The State of Psychotherapy Today," in the *Zentralblatt* in February 1934, Jung made some unsupportable statements. "The Jews have this peculiarity in common with women; being physically weaker, they have to aim at the chinks in the armour of their adversary.... The Jew, who is something of a nomad, has never yet created a cultural form of his own and as far as we can see never will, since all his instincts and talents require a more or less civilized nation to act as host for their development" (Jung 1934b, para. 353). Some critics have seen some anti-Semitism in Jung's statements. Gilman (1993) is an intelligent example (pp. 31-32). Samuels (1993), also an intelligent example, saw some similarities with Nazi notions concerning Jews, particularly regarding nation and national difference (pp. 292-93, 318).

On 27 February 1934 Gustav Bally, a psychoanalyst who had fled from Germany to Switzerland, criticized Jung in the *Neue Zuercher Zeitung*. In his article, "'*Deutschstaemmige*' Psychotherapie?" ("'German-born' Psychotherapy?"), he argued that Jung's association with the GMSP and editorship of the *Zentralblatt* had legitimized the Nazi view of Germanic psychology and psychiatry. Jung's distinction between Jewish and Germanic traits in his December editorial in the *Zentralblatt* lacked reasonable proof. Bally warned that a person who introduced himself as editor with the racial question should be aware that his statements appeared against a background of organized passion that would color the interpretation of his words (Bally 1934, cited in Bair 2003, p. 451). Lammers (2012a) pointed out that when Jung made statements concerning race and Jews in the *Zentralblatt* in December 1933 and February 1934, his language had, at that moment in history, "a painful resonance" (pp. 111-12). Lammers (2012b) noted further that Jung's editorial seemed racist to Bally at the time, but that he related to Jung later as a trusted colleague (pp. 76, 83n.4).

Transition in Jung's views during spring 1934

Soon after the appearance of Bally's article, Erich Neumann—who was Jewish, had left Germany for Zurich in September 1933, and is often described as one of Jung's most talented students—wrote to Jung. He said he had spoken in some dismay with Toni Wolff about the partial validity of Bally's article, and she had given him Jung's article "The State of Psychotherapy Today." He remarked that he knew he did not have to tell Jung what he meant to him and how hard it was for him to disagree with Jung, but he felt he "simply must take issue with you on a matter that goes far beyond any merely personal concerns." He said he could not comprehend why a person like Jung could not see what was all too obvious: that in the shadow-side in the Germanic psyche "a mind-numbing cloud of filth, blood and rottenness is brewing." He continued that "where I come from, great men have always been called upon to exercise discernment and to stand against the crowd." Moreover, Neumann "would wish to disabuse you of the conviction that Jews are as you imagine them to be." Despite the fact that Jung treated some Jews, "from where, dear Dr. Jung, do you know the Jewish race, the Jewish people?" Furthermore, Neumann asked, was there not "a misunderstanding in a sentence such as: 'The Aryan unconscious has a higher potential than the Jewish [one] . . .'" in Jung's article, "The State of Psychotherapy Today." On the contrary, Neumann said, the Hasidic movement and Zionism "demonstrate the inexhaustible liveliness of the Jewish people," and he gave as examples "the renaissance of the Hebrew language that was dead for 2,000 years and the settlement in Palestine." This Jewish renaissance seemed to him "to be more embryonic, youthful, and full of energy than the Nazi-rigid, brutally organized and stolid, extreme submissiveness of the Aryan revivals." What did it imply, he asked, that Jung had told him that all bad instincts had been called upon in Bolshevism, but, in Jung's view, it was different in Germany? Neumann stated that he believed and learned from Jung that "the most precious secret of every human being" was, "in essence, the purely creative prescient depths of one's soul." He commented that he did not wish to change anything he had written in his present letter. Hopefully Jung would "appreciate how it is intended." Neumann concluded that precisely his gratitude toward Jung "obliges me to be candid" (Neumann 1934). Apparently, Jung and Neumann then talked about the matter, and there is no letter of reply by Jung to Neumann's letter either before or after Neumann's departure for Palestine in May.

Jung's reply to Bally's article appeared in the *Neue Zuercher Zeitung* on 13-14 March. He wrote that as conditions were, a stroke of the pen in high places in Germany would have swept all psychotherapy there under the table. This had to be prevented for the sake of humanity, doctors, and science. Thus Jung had accepted the GMSP's presidency and editorship of its *Zentralblatt*. Science had to preserve its intellectual heritage under the changed conditions. Regarding Matthias Goering's statement, Jung had thought that Cimbal, managing editor of the *Zentralblatt*, would bring out a special issue with a statement by Goering, head of the German section of the GMSP, for circulation in Germany only. To Jung's surprise and disappointment Goering's statement was printed in the December issue of the *Zentralblatt*. In this way Jung's name appeared over a National Socialist manifesto, which to him personally was anything but agreeable. In the same issue Jung, in his editorial, wrote of the difference between Jewish and Germanic psychology. If he were in the position—as Bally supposed him to be—of being unable to point to a single difference between these two psychologies, it would be tantamount to being unable to make plausible differences between English and American or French and German psychologies. Jung had not invented these differences. One could read about them in numerous books and newspapers. Psychological differences existed between all nations and races, and even in Switzerland between inhabitants of Zurich, Bern, and Basel. All branches of humankind united in one stem, but a stem had separate branches. But, readers might object, why raise the question of a Jewish psychology now and in Germany of all places? Jung responded that he had raised it long ago, not just now (Jung 1934c, paras. 1017, 1020-21, 1025, 1028-29, 1034). Nevertheless, Jung's reply to Bally left unanswered Bally's point that one who introduced himself as editor with the racial question should be aware that his statements appeared against a background of organized passion that would color the interpretation of his words.

We believe that Bally's criticisms in the newspaper in Zurich, Jung's hometown, and perhaps Neumann's letter to Jung made Jung aware of a danger to him and his reputation in being unwary of the Nazis and of statements that might seem anti-Semitic. Soon after Bally's article he entered into a transition in March 1934 in which he became warier both of the Nazis and of anti-Semitic statements.

On 2 March, Jung wrote to Cimbal, J.H. van der Hoop, a leader among Dutch psychotherapists, and Oluf Bruel, a leader among Danish psychotherapists, expressing his displeasure that Goering's statement had appeared in the *Zentralblatt's* December issue, not just in a special German issue. Still he did not want to hold Cimbal or Goering personally responsible for this, as they were under domestic political pressure (Jung 1973, pp. 144-47).

A hitherto unpublished letter by van der Hoop to Jung on 4 March informed Jung of a very significant recent meeting of the Dutch Society for Psychotherapy. Van der Hoop said that many questions were raised that he could not answer because the structure of the International GMSP was still uncertain. As foreigners the Dutch "have naturally little desire to become politically coordinated [to the German government]," and should most members of the International GMSP—*i.e.,* the German members—have to live under such an arrangement, it would not be easy to keep out the influence of political coordination. Van der Hoop then asked some very pertinent questions: Could some "German psychotherapists be members of the International Society without being members in the German national group?" Would the International Society "have only ties to the national groups or also to individual members?" Would it not be important that we "formulate our wishes for a structure of the International Society?" We would wish "that the membership of the International Society would not be bound by conditions of race, religion, or political view." Should the German national group demand a certain world view of its members, we would want such a limitation not to be valid for German members of the International Society. We would further wish "that the directorship of the International Society be elected in such a way that the German Society could exert no all domineering influence." Van der Hoop said he would be pleased to have Jung's opinion about these wishes for the structuring of the International Society. Jung could view his letter "as an expression of the position of the Dutch Society." He hoped very much that Jung would succeed in creating a firm structure, and he would be pleased should he be able to help Jung in this (van der Hoop 1934a). Van der Hoop's wonderful letter of 4 March was indeed very helpful to Jung!

On 12 March Jung replied in answer to van der Hoop's questions. Jung stated that it goes without saying that the International Society was totally independent of the German group, which could not exist without being conformed—a necessity that applied "only inside Germany." Though the International Society would consist of separate national groups, the necessity would arise of accepting "individual members who do not belong to any national group." At present, no regulations existed about this as Jung had not yet worked out the statutes for the International GMSP. He intended, however, "to carry through this work at the next Congress" for Psychotherapy in Bad Nauheim in May. The International Society could "accept any kind of member. Race, religion, and suchlike things are not taken into account, nor of course political sentiments." To keep the large number of German members from a decisive voice in the International Society's conduct, it would be necessary that the national societies "nominate some kind of representatives or delegates. In this way it will be possible to paralyze in a constitutive assembly what might [otherwise] be an overwhelming German influence." Since the Germans had a great interest in getting affiliated abroad, Jung thought they would not "make special difficulties." At any rate it "is worth trying." Jung would propose that individual psychotherapists regardless of where they came from be allowed membership in the International Society. He told van der Hoop that he was very grateful for his positive cooperation, without which the complicated situation could not be coped with in a fruitful way (Jung 1934d; Jung 1973, pp. 149-51). Jung then consulted Vladimir Rosenbaum, his lawyer in Zurich who was Jewish, and they worked out the draft of statutes for ratification at the Congress in Bad Nauheim, Germany in early May. See Bair (2003) for an excellent account of Jung's consultation with Rosenbaum (pp. 448-50). These statutes enabled Jewish German psychotherapists to become members of the International GMSP.

In a letter of 9 April, van der Hoop told Jung that "your detailed letter of 12 March has clarified the situation very much for me. It pleases me to see that our views agree on many points." He hoped that they would have a fruitful collaboration. He understood that the leadership was not easy for Jung (van der Hoop 1934b).

On 20 April 1934, Jung wrote Heyer that, since their motives and interests were so obscure that an outsider like him could not see through them, Jung could not rely on Cimbal and Goering

(Jung 1934e; Jung 1973, p. 158). This is quite a contrast to his view in November 1933 that Goering was a very amiable and reasonable man!

In addition to the ratification of Jung's new statutes at the Bad Nauheim Congress in May, Jung delivered a lecture there, "On Complex Theory," in which he paid tribute to Freud as a psychological pioneer who had explored the unconscious and put forth the first medical theory of the unconscious (Jung 1934f, p. 141). Jung's favorable comments on Freud angered Nazis. This is a contrast to Jung's comments regarding Freud in his letters to Kranefeldt, 20 December 1933 and 9 February 1934, cited above. Finally, later that May, Jung informed James Kirsch, an analytical psychologist then in Palestine, that his new book *Wirklichkeit der Seele (Reality of the Soul)* had been published. Jung had included an essay by Hugo Rosenthal, a Jewish author, "Der Typengegensatz in der juedischen Religionsgeschichte" ("Opposite types in Jewish religious history"), to annoy the Nazis, on the one hand, and those who decried him as an anti-Semite, on the other (Jung 1934g). He had made a transition in his views during the spring of 1934.

We will conclude by pointing out that Jung himself, looking back after the end of World War II in Europe on his views of Nazi Germany, implied on two occasions in 1945 that his views had changed in 1934. In his article "After the Catastrophe," published in June 1945, Jung wrote: "But we must not forget that we are judging from today, from a knowledge of the events which led to the catastrophe. Our judgment would certainly be very different had our information stopped short at 1933 or 1934. At that time, in Germany as well as in Italy, there were not a few things that appeared plausible and seemed to speak in favour of the regime."

He gave as an example "the disappearance of the unemployed, who used to tramp the German highroads in their hundreds of thousands" (Jung 1945c/1970, par. 420). In a letter to Mary Mellon on 24 September 1945 responding to allegations in the U.S. that he was a Nazi sympathizer, Jung said that he had "challenged the Nazis already in 1934 at a great reception in Frankfort in the house of Baron von Schnitzler, the Director of the I.G. Farben concern. I told them that their anticlockwise Swastika is whirling down into the abyss of unconsciousness and evil" (Jung 1945e). We note that Jung here wrote specifically that he had "challenged the Nazis already in 1934"—he did not write "in 1933."

Chapter 2
From 1934 to Nazi Germany's Invasion of Poland (1939)

After Nazi Germany's first year it is untenable to hold that Jung was a "Nazi sympathizer." This chapter first shows that his wariness of the Nazis increased from 1934 to 1936. By March 1936 his attitude toward them took a further turn: it was clearly more *pessimistic* than a year earlier in 1935.

The mid-1930s: 1934-1936

In the mid-1930s Jung saw Germany in terms of archetypes. In his Visions Seminar in March 1934, for example, Jung said that, for ancient Egypt, the Pharoah was Egypt and Egypt was the Pharoah and that this kind of psychology still existed: you could read in newspapers that Hitler was Germany and Germany was Hitler. A member of Jung's seminar remarked: like Louis XIV of France. Jung replied yes, this kind of psychology was archetypal, which explained the extent to which a whole people could project the idea of the individual Self onto one ideal (Jung 1934h/1976, 484).

Looking back at 1934, Jung wrote to van der Hoop in the Netherlands that, in his opinion, a sufficiently international beginning had been made for the International GMSP. Although it did not at present include national groups from all pertinent European countries, that was certainly not their fault (19 January 1935, Jung 1973, 185). Delegates from Switzerland, the Netherlands, Germany, Denmark, and Sweden had ratified the new statutes at Bad Nauheim.

A session of Jung's 1935 seminar on Nietzsche's *Zarathustra* on 13 February illustrates his continued uncertainty toward the Nazi movement. At a request from the audience Jung addressed the "backward" movement of the Nazi swastika. He suggested that the movement of the swastika to the left was not so much a "backward" movement as a wrong movement. Despite his negative language, he added that although to an outsider, the swastika moved the wrong way, if one put oneself into the swastika, it appeared to move the right way. He concluded his musings by saying that it had a psychological meaning, of whatever kind, so he thought it really meant something that it moved the wrong way (Jung 1935b/1988, 373).

In the same seminar session, Jung postulated that the "backward" movement of the swastika coincided with the transition from the Age of Pisces into the Age of Aquarius—a transition in human attitudes. He saw this in mass movements throughout the world. Jung said that there was only a slight difference between Communism and National Socialism. Moreover, he saw the same movement in Roosevelt's New Deal; it was, at its core, the same thing. This remark was very sweeping and inaccurate. But it suggests that Jung had placed Nazism within a broad context of world-wide change—as he described it, a sort of low-level collectivity. Jung viewed political events as being shaped by the unconscious, and here he saw National Socialism as a component of a collective shift on a massive scale (Jung 1935b/1988, 376).

A comment from the audience during the 13 February seminar is worth discussing. Mrs. Martha Sigg commented that she thought one could have optimistic ideas about the black color of the Nazi swastika, which Jung had just before associated with evil. Jung responded that we were not judges; we simply made statements. It seems that he wanted to assess the situation through the theoretical lens of his psychology of archetypes. Next he said: there was nothing so evil that out of it something good could not come. Jung was not completely ruling out the possibility of some positive outcome from the Nazi government, nor was he taking an oppositional position toward it. After his response, Sigg suggested to him that to jump further, one must fall back (that is, any temporary regression under Nazism would be for the eventual good of Germany). Jung replied cautiously that there were certain backward jumps in history when no better jump followed (Jung 1935b/1988, 377-78). Though not ruling out the possibility of some positive outcome, his statements, taken together in this 13 February seminar session, offer evidence that he was taking a more negative view of Nazi Germany.

Jung was hardly alone in 1935 in being uncertain of how Nazi Germany would go down in history. No less a figure than Winston Churchill wrote in 1935 that we could not tell whether Hitler would be the person who loosed on the world another war destroying civilization or who restored honor to Germany and returned it into the forefront of Europe's family circle (Churchill 1937/1942, 195).

On 22 May 1935, Jung spoke further about unconscious forces moving Germany. He said that some people were having pagan experiences that, if experienced alone by individuals, might be relatively harmless. But their systematic organization at a conscious level would be dangerous, and this systematic organization was happening in Germany (Jung 1935b/1988, 501). This seminar session evidences Jung's perception of archetypal forces in Germany heading in a negative direction.

Later in 1935, Jung delivered a series of lectures to the Tavistock Clinic in London. On 12 March 1935 he had written to Kranefeldt that the Tavistock Clinic had invited him and that he would rather not go as he already had enough work on the docket; were he to go it would not be before October (Jung 1935c). In any event, he went to deliver the lectures from 30 September to 4 October. We note that in Lecture V he said that both Italy and Germany were dealing with the savior complex as mass psychology. The people of both countries were projecting this archetypal image onto human savior figures—specifically Mussolini and Hitler. Again, Jung displayed an archetypal approach to viewing current events. He went on to note that the savior complex quite naturally became activated in an era so full of trouble and disorientation as their own. Later in the lecture, Jung posed this question: who in 1900 would have thought that approximately thirty years later, an archetype would seize a whole nation—Germany—of intelligent and cultivated people? Jung concluded that one could not say it was right or wrong. It had nothing to do with rational judgment; it was just history. Given an archetype, the people and whole crowd moved like one person; there was no resisting it (Jung 1935d/1976, paras. 369, 372).

From 1934 to Nazi Germany's Invasion of Poland (1939)

In March 1936, Jung published his essay "Wotan." Maintaining an archetypal view of Germany under National Socialism, he suggested—wrongly, in our opinion—that the archetype of Wotan, the Germanic god of storm and frenzy, better explained the Nazi movement than political, economic, and psychological factors did. Jung thought that an archetypal influence had seized Germans, young and old; they were becoming possessed. Jung asserted that unless one wished to deify Hitler, which had happened, the Wotan archetype was really the only explanation for the fury that had come over Germany. Wotan, according to Jung, also affected and possessed the leader exalted by the German public. Jung stated that Hitler, who was clearly possessed, had possessed a whole people to the extent that everything had been set in motion and had begun rolling, embarked on a dangerous course (Jung 1936a/1970, *CW* 10, paras. 385-88; Sherry 2010, 147). These comments show that Jung remained invested in an archetypal theory. However, we further note that Jung also spoke specifically in strong language about Hitler's role in the matter: Hitler, himself possessed, had possessed the German people and was leading them on a dangerous course. Although we accept Sherry's correction of R.F.C. Hull's translation, we obviously disagree with his opinion that by 1936 Jung had not formed a more critical view of Nazi Germany than he previously had. In 1933, Jung did not know whether the Nazi movement might bring some new thing of value into the world or just carry off people to their madness. By March 1936, he thought the latter was occurring.

Later in "Wotan," Jung constructed an analogy in which he compared a nation under an archetypal force to a rushing river that human reason could not control. Human control came to an end when the individual was caught in a mass movement. Here, however, a question of responsibility arises. The way in which Jung described Germany under archetypal influence seems to take responsibility off of individuals in Germany. Did he think that Germans had little responsibility for what was happening in their country? Near the close of his essay he suggested that Germans should not be judged so much as responsible agents but perhaps regarded also as victims. He recognized Germany was headed in a negative direction. But because he based his explanation on an archetype, he hesitated to place responsibility. In conclusion, he suggested that Wotan's reawakening, which Germany was currently witnessing, was a step backward, but one that would not last forever. He speculated that Nazism would "not be the last word" that the archetype would reveal.

This conclusion is telling in two ways. First, it seems Jung was now clearer in his views of Nazi Germany: it was the stormy and violent negative aspect that derived from the archetype of Wotan. Second, despite this negative view of Nazi Germany, Jung retained an uncertain hope for Germany in the next "years or decades" (Jung 1936a/1970, *CW* 10, paras. 395, 398-99). We accept the view of Dohe (2016) that "Jung suggested that the Germans were capable of a collective spiritual rebirth." But we disagree with the statement "that Jung saw National Socialism as a potential individuation process *en masse*" (Dohe, p. 13). As we have shown, by spring 1934 Jung had become warier of the Nazis. By March 1936 his attitude toward the Nazis had taken a further turn: it was clearly more pessimistic than a year earlier in 1935, although he still maintained that an archetype was behind the movement in Germany.

After Jung published "Wotan" in March 1936, he was satisfied with the view of Nazi Germany at which he had arrived: the stormy, violent negative aspect that derived from the Wotan archetype (Jung 1936a/1970, para. 399). Nevertheless, a controversy occurred in the *Harvard Crimson* in the United States in 1936 when Harvard University invited Jung to receive an honorary doctoral degree in September. The *Crimson* printed an excerpt from his editorial in the *Zentralblatt fuer Psychotherapie*, VI, December 1933 and suggested that it showed Nazi sentiments: "The differences between Germanic and Jewish psychology which have been known to exist for a long time to people of insight must no longer be disguised. This will be an advantage to science." Dr. Henry A. Murray, assistant professor of psychology at Harvard, replied in the *Crimson*: he pointed out that Jung had held the opinion that racial differences exist for many years before 1933, when Hitler became Chancellor of Germany. Moreover, Murray included the significant sentence which the excerpt had omitted: "Therefore, as I [Jung] should like to state clearly, there shall be no inferiority of the Semitic psychology implied, any more than such is implied of the Chinese, when the psychology peculiar to that Oriental people is under discussion" (Murray 1936). Murray concluded that Jung here showed he did not subscribe to Nazi race theories. The controversy did not prevent Harvard from awarding Jung the honorary doctorate. On Jung at Harvard, William G. Barrett, who had an analysis with Jung but who became a Freudian in his psychiatric practice, commented that he had early on felt that Jung was disappointed in not having a larger following among psychiatrists; upon reflecting on it, Barrett came to believe that his conclusion was right (Barrett 1969, p. 13).

Jung's Evolving Views of Nazi Germany

In his article, "The State of Psychotherapy Today" in the *Zentralblatt fuer Psychotherapie* in 1934, Jung had made some unsupportable statements: "The Jews have this peculiarity in common with women; being physically weaker, they have to aim at the chinks in the armour of their adversary . . . The Jew, who is something of a nomad, has never yet created a cultural form of his own and as far as we can see never will, since all his instincts and talents require a more or less civilized nation to act as host for their development" (Jung 1934b, para. 353). Some critics saw anti-Semitism in Jung's statements: Gilman (1993, pp. 31-32) is an intelligent recent example. Samuels (1993) saw some similarities with Nazi notions concerning Jews, particularly regarding nation and national difference (pp. 292-93, 318).

Some critics, however, went further and suggested that Jung had Nazi sympathies. Frosh (2005), for instance, wrote that antagonism to Freud and Jung's general opportunism fueled Jung's anti-Semitism, that "Jungianism's theoretical base" left it open to racist concepts, and that this was indicative of a more widespread phenomenon. Many psychotherapists, including some psycho-analysts as well as Jung, showed admiration for Hitler's leadership and for Germany finding its destiny through Nazism. For Jung and at least some psychoanalysts, the question was not just one of preserving depth psychology in Germany but also of finding a place for psychotherapy in a system that promoted nationalism and authority; individuals disappeared in the mass and their only value was what they might contribute to national revival. This excited some participants, Jungian and psychoanalytic alike, and they sided with the mass (Frosh 2005, pp. 268-69).

On the contrary, as we have seen in Chapters 1-2 of the present book, it is untenable to hold that Jung was a Nazi sympathizer after Nazi Germany's first year!

From Fall 1936 to Hitler's invasion of Poland (September 1939)

Jung in his own view saw himself as scientific in his psychological views and nonpolitical in his approach. After receiving the honorary degree at Harvard, he replied on 29 September 1936 to a letter from Abraham Aaron Roback, a Jewish American psychologist by saying that he was not a Nazi sympathizer and was quite nonpolitical. He further stated that since 1917, he had maintained that there was a difference between Jewish and Christian psychology and that some Jewish authors had done the same. He said that he was no anti-Semite (Jung 1973, p. 219).

In a lecture delivered on 14 October 1936 at the Tavistock Clinic in London, Jung made his strongest and most negative statements to that date about Nazi Germany and Hitler. Jung suggested that we find the psychological symptoms of the epoch chiefly in those nations mangled the most by war, misery, and insecurity (Jung 1936b/1976, paras. 1322-23). Through National Socialism in Germany, Communism in the Soviet Union, and Fascism in Italy, the State became all-powerful and claimed slaves body and soul. It voiced a totalitarian point of view: one sheep was as good as another, but plain-clothed and uniformed wolf-dogs guarded the herd, crowded together and utterly deprived of all rights. Only duties, no rights, were left. The new slave owner, the State, sucked up every source of energy (ibid., para. 1324). The new leaders said: "I am the State." The State incarnated itself in these men who had been inconspicuous nobodies previously, but equipped with a great voice that cowed the people into obedience (ibid., para. 1325). This process of incarnation was particularly drastic in Hitler's case. When the State spoke through him, he spoke with a voice of thunder and swept together crowds of millions (ibid., para. 1326). Germany showed an underlying archetypical symbolism produced by the eruption of the collective unconscious. Wotanistic symbolism, Indo-Germanic speculation, etc. were found in neo-paganism in Germany (ibid., para. 1329). When Friedrich Nietzsche had written *Thus Spoke Zarathustra* (1883-91), he had no notion that the superman he created out of his personal misery would be a prophetic anticipation of a Fuehrer or Duce. Hitler and Mussolini were ordinary human beings who assumed that they themselves knew what to do in a situation practically nobody understood (op. cit., para. 1333). To people compulsory order seemed preferable to the terrors of chaos, the lesser of two evils (ibid., para 1340). These negative views regarding Nazi Germany and Hitler in this unpublished lecture at the Tavistock Clinic, London, in October 1936, were stronger and more negative than the views he had expressed in his lectures there from 30 September to 4 October 1935.

Nevertheless, Jung would refrain from expressing views close to politics at meetings of the International General Medical Society for Psychotherapy (hereafter abbreviated IGMSP), of which he was president. To Oluf Bruel, a leader among Danish psychotherapists, Jung commented on 12 December that the general political atmosphere precluded introducing any topic near to politics at meetings of the IGMSP (Jung 1973, p. 221).

From 1934 to Nazi Germany's Invasion of Poland (1939)

Looking back in 1945, Jung wrote that his observations of Hitler had led him in 1937 to conclude that should the catastrophe of war come, it would be far bloodier than he had previously supposed, for Hitler, a "theatrical hysteric," had by 1937 the armored divisions of the Wehrmacht and German heavy industry's weight behind him (Jung 1945c/1970, para. 419). In September 1937, Jung was in Berlin to give lectures to the C.G. Jung *Gesellschaft*. While there, he attended a parade reviewing troops and weapons that enabled him to observe Hitler and Mussolini. He commented to the members of the *Gesellschaft*: out there, archetypes were already walking in the streets (Bair 2003, p. 456).

In October 1937, Jung gave the Terry Lectures at Yale University. Twice in the Lectures he made striking comments about Nazi Germany. First, with Nazi Germany and the Soviet Union in mind, he remarked that we now witnessed the amazing spectacle of states taking over claims of theocracy, that is, of totality and suppressing free opinion. Again people slew each other to support childish theories of producing heaven on earth. The powers of the underworld were now creating, or attempting to create, a state slavery and prison with no mental or spiritual charm. Later in the Lectures, he commented: if a person declared God dead, then he or she should find out to where this considerable energy, once invested in God, had disappeared. It might reappear under another name such as "Wotan" or "state'" or some "-ism" [for example, National Socialism or Communism], of which people believed and expected as much as they previously had of God (Jung 1937/1938, pp. 59, 104). Jung, when speaking, could be blunt at times. In 1940 a German version of Jung's Terry Lectures appeared. When Matthias Goering, head of the German section of the IGMSP, got wind of Jung's Terry Lectures and his interview by H. R. Knickerbocker in *Hearst's International-Cosmopolitan*, January 1939—which we shall soon discuss—Bair (2003) says that Jung's name was placed on the *Schwarze Liste* (Black List) of writers banned in Germany. His *Essais de Psychologie Analytique* was placed on the Otto List, the French equivalent of the Black List, after France fell (Bair 2003, pp. 462, 800).

His increasingly negative views of Nazi Germany notwithstanding, Jung still hoped in early 1938 to keep the IGMSP's congresses nonpolitical. On 26 March 1938, he wrote to Eric Benjamin Strauss, an English psychiatrist, about the upcoming IGMSP Congress at Oxford, 29 July–2 August. Jung stated that he could not and would not exclude non-Aryan speakers—for example, Jewish speakers. The only condition on which he insisted was that everyone, Aryan or non-Aryan, refrain from remarks likely to arouse "the political psychosis" of the times. Should a speaker trespass this limit, Jung as President would stop him or her immediately. To Jung a scientific Congress was not a "place to indulge in political follies" (Jung 1973, p. 242). Moreover, he had prevented a main topic on race proposed by Goering for the Congress (Sorge 2012, p. 41).

At the Oxford Congress in summer 1938, a radical shift in the balance in the IGMSP occurred: first, the English national group, with some 150 members, was founded and became the second largest group, next to Germany. Secondly, the IGMSP elected Hugh Crichton-Miller, co-founder of the Tavistock Clinic, London, as vice president. Goering, who had aspired to the office, took Crichton-Miller's election as a betrayal. He was also angered by the election of Strauss, who was Jewish, as president of the English group. Goering protested that Germany was being edged out of the leading position on the board, but Jung said that the election of a vice president should not be interpreted as a political gesture (Sorge 2012, p. 42).

In fall 1938 very important political events occurred in Europe. The Sudetenland Crisis threatened war. Britain and France at the Munich Conference avoided war by ceding the Sudetenland to Germany. Jung, relieved that war had been averted, wrote to Ruth Bailey, a good friend in England, that the Prime Minister of Britain, Neville Chamberlain, was a great statesman (Jung 1938a). While Jung might have held this view immediately after the Munich Conference, historians today, of course, do not regard Chamberlain as a great statesman.

In an interview by the American journalist H.R. Knicker-bocker in October 1938 in Kuesnacht for an article in *Hearst's International-Cosmopolitan*, Jung made strong statements on Hitler and Nazi Germany. He analyzed Hitler as "medicine man" and voice of a German collective unconscious. First, he said two types of strong men existed in primitive society: the chief who was physically powerful and the medicine man who was strong not in himself but by the power people projected onto him. Hitler's body did not suggest physical strength. He belonged in the category of medicine man. Jung went on to point to the revival of the cult of Wotan in Germany. Wotan was the god of wind. Jung saw the name Storm Troops as an example—storm suggested wind. The swastika was another symbol: it was a revolving vortex moving toward the left—which meant sinister, unfavorable, and directed toward the unconscious. These symbols of a Third Reich led by Hitler, its prophet, under banners of storm, wind, and whirling vortices, pointed to a mass movement sweeping the German people on and on in unreasoning emotion to a destiny perhaps no one could foresee (Jung 1938b/1977, pp. 115-18).

Jung next suggested that Hitler regarded himself as the voice of Germans' unconscious. He was the loudspeaker that magnified the inaudible whispers of the German psyche. His secret was twofold: his unconscious had exceptional access to his consciousness, and he let himself be moved by it and acted upon it. Since their defeat in World War I, Germans had awaited a Savior. Hitler's first idea was to make his people powerful. Jung added that Hitler believed the Aryan German spirit deserved to be supported by might, muscle, and steel. Hitler as a man hardly existed: he disappeared behind his role. Jung concluded that with Hitler you were scared. You could never talk to him because nobody was there. He was not a man, but a collective; not an individual, but a nation (Jung 1938b/1977, pp. 118-19, 122, 124, 126, 128).

Lastly, Jung, as a physician, recommended a treatment of Hitler. He said that it was extremely difficult and excessively dangerous to deal with such a man acting under compulsion. Hitler's unconscious voice told him to unite the German people and lead them toward a bigger place on earth and a position of glory and richness. Nothing could stop him from attempting to do that. One might hope, however, to influence the direction of his expansion. Jung said: let him go East. Encourage him to keep his attention turned away from the West: let him go to Russia. Indeed, in June 1941 Nazi Germany invaded the Soviet Union. Jung predicted that Hitler would not keep Germany's word against its interest in any agreement or treaty (Jung 1938b/1977, pp. 131-32, 134). The prediction would prove to be correct. This interview in

October 1938 was published in *Hearst's International-Cosmopolitan* in January 1939.

On the night of 9/10 November 1938, *Kristallnacht* occurred in Germany. Nazis destroyed Jewish synagogues and properties, beat up many Jews and killed some. In a letter to Erich Neumann on 19 December, Jung in Kuesnacht said that everyone there was profoundly shaken by what was happening in Germany. Jung was quite involved in helping Jewish refugees and worked toward bringing Jewish acquaintances to safety in Britain and America (Jung 1973, p. 251).

After the Sudetenland Crisis had threatened war, Jung in interviews made stronger comments on Hitler and Nazi Germany. Having seen the interview of Jung in *Hearst's Cosmopolitan* of January 1939, Howard L. Philp, a clergyman and psychologist in England, interviewed Jung in April 1939. In March 1939, Hitler, breaking his word, had taken the rest of Czechoslovakia, and Britain had given a guarantee to Poland. Philp asked Jung what effect the latter would have on Hitler. Jung answered that was difficult to foresee. Hitler voiced what he wanted and got it. As in the *Cosmopolitan* interview, Jung said that Hitler fell into the class of the medicine man, that Germans had looked to him as their savior, and that he was what Germans had made him. He told Philp that Hitler did not understand himself, but he had an uncanny power of being sensitive to the collective unconscious in Germany. Hitler regarded himself as the nation. And the nation did not keep its word. Jung went on to say that Hitler never had a healthy relationship to his anima. He was possessed by it. He was consequently destructive, not creative. This was a reason why he was dangerous; he did not have the seeds of harmony within himself. Jung did not think Hitler would cease to be abnormal. He predicted that Hitler would probably die in his job (Jung 1939a/1977, pp. 136-40). This prediction turned out to be correct. In a seminar talk to the Guild of Pastoral Psychology, London, on 5 April 1939, Jung said that the emotion in Germany was warlike. Hitler and other Germans were drunk with a wild god [Wotan] (Jung 1939b/1976, para. 639).

On 28 June 1939, Jung wrote to Hugh Crichton-Miller, the vice president of the IGMSP, that he wanted to withdraw as President (Jung 1973, p. 272). He had served in the position since 1933. At the meeting of delegates in Zurich in July, he tendered his resignation. But he was induced to remain President until such time as the applications of new national groups (Italy, Hungary, and Japan) for admission had been dealt with (Jung 1973, pp. 272n., 286). He was looking for a successor from a neutral country to minimize tension between the Allied and Axis national groups. Crichton-Miller had suggested van der Hoop, the leader of the Dutch national group, but Matthias Goering interpreted the suggestion as a slight to Germany. Replying to Crichton-Miller on 2 September—one day after Hitler invaded Poland—Jung wrote that Goering's misinterpretation of Crichton-Miller's suggestion had everything to do with Goering's general inability and nothing to do with his inability to understand English. Should Crichton-Miller suspect Goering of foolish prestige motives he would not be far from the truth. Nazi Germany had invaded Poland, and the devil knew how the world might look should they ever meet again. Jung concluded that Hitler was reaching his climax along with the German psychosis (Jung 1973, pp. 275-76).

From 1934 to Nazi Germany's Invasion of Poland (1939)

World War II began with Nazi Germany's invasion of Poland in September 1939. On 28 September, Jung wrote to Esther Harding, an analytical psychologist in New York City who would later in 1944-45 defend him against allegations of having been a Nazi sympathizer (Schoenl 2009). Jung told Harding that the Swiss naturally hoped not to be involved in the war, but that if it had to be, it would be on the Allies' side. After Nazi Germany's invasion of Poland, Jung said that the conviction existed in Switzerland that Germany had lost its national honor to an unspeakable degree (Jung 1939c).

Chapter 3
The World War II Years: 1939-1945

Chapter 3 will show how strongly anti-Nazi Jung's views were in relation to events during World War II such as the fall of France, the bombings of Britain, the U.S. entry into the war, and Allied troops advancing into Germany. It will also show the beginnings and development of allegations in 1944 in the United States that Jung was pro-Nazi. Esther Harding and Eleanor Bertine, two prominent Jungian psychologists in New York City, kept Jung informed of the allegations. This chapter demonstrates Jung's evolving views from 1939 to the war's end in 1945.

Jung's strongly anti-Nazi views in relation to events during the war

On 4 November 1939, Jung wrote Harding that he believed that Hitler had an inclination to keep strong in order to push the Soviet Union back as soon as the trouble in Western Europe was settled. A woman acquainted with a Swiss family wrote how sad it was that her husband in the German army had been killed in Poland, but she added: "Thank God, my Fuehrer lives." Jung commented: it sounded exactly like "my Savior liveth." He remarked: the worst of it was that Hitler had a "religious" prestige and that some people disbelieved he was responsible for the evil things that they could not deny. They attributed them to bad underlings of whom Hitler was unaware (Jung 1939d).

On 26 February 1940, Jung wrote Harding that it was appalling to see how Germany's cultural level was rapidly sinking because of the suffocation of free thought. How the Germans dealt with Poland and Czechoslovakia was well-known outside Germany. Everybody around Germany knew what was in store should Germany win the war (Jung 1940a).

In April, the war—quiet during the winter—erupted. Norway and Denmark were invaded, and German military forces prepared to invade the Low Countries and France.

When France fell, Jung—fearing that communications with the United States would be cut off—wrote his friend and patient Mary Mellon on 19 June that night had descended on Europe (Jung 1940b). On his friendship with her, see Schoenl (1998); much of the Jung-Mary Mellon correspondence appeared in this book. Due to the fear of a German invasion, Jung temporarily moved his family to the Swiss Alps. On 21 August, he gave Mary his perceptions of conditions in Switzerland and in Europe. The Swiss government had advised people to lay in stores of food: if they would eat one-fifth less, Switzerland could support itself. There would be no shortage of milk and meat unless Germany invaded. The Swiss were afraid that Germany might destroy them. The current German mentality was thoroughly irrational and mystical. Reason was not the criterion by which it could be understood. The Third Reich was mistakenly in quest of an everlasting kingdom on earth. People like that were miserable and spread misery. In contrast, Jung believed a kingdom could be conquered only within—not on the map of Europe. He saw a good number of French interned in Switzerland. He thought that France's fall had been a moral crash on the part of France. He concluded by writing that Europeans were now in prison: God save our souls (Jung 1940c). In response to her gift of records of black spirituals, Jung wrote to Mary Mellon in October, adding that the world suffered from Nazi Germany's outburst of insanity. He thought it might suspend every reasonable communication for years (Jung 1940d).

In January 1941, Jung told Mary that Germany's air war against Britain and the destruction of France were almost more than one could bear. The bombings' devastation of London had hurt Jung as if Britain were his own country. It was now a question whether they in Europe could keep the treasures of culture against the onslaught by the powers of darkness. In Switzerland, things were as if frozen. People still moved about in the streets and trains ran but automobiles had nearly vanished. Everything cost more, though food was still plentiful. The Swiss military concentrated in the Alps in case of a German invasion but the lower land would have to be sacrificed. Although invasion of Switzerland would be madness, the Germans were mad. The Swiss sympathies were on the British side. Though Jung had heard that the mood in the German army had dropped since Britain could not be conquered, the young people in Germany were still full of illusions. Should Switzerland come under German domination, Jung would certainly be silenced. He hoped, however, that this would not happen and that he would see Mary again (Jung 1941).

Japan's attack on Pearl Harbor brought the United States into World War II but the following year, 1942, was a difficult year for the Allies. Jung wrote to Mary Mellon in January 1942 that, at least as experienced in Switzerland, the European condition was indescribable. Hellish suspense existed, and everything was provisional. Life moved forward like a ticking clock that could not be wound again (Jung 1942a). In a letter of 10 April 1942, Jung told Esther Harding that the situation in Europe was getting blacker and blacker. It was great news when they heard that the United States had been brought into the war albeit through the tragic attacks on Pearl Harbor. It stirred people in the U.S. from their slumber and unconsciousness. They in Europe had been seriously afraid that America would enter too late (Jung 1942b). To Mary Mellon on the same date, Jung, in commenting on his own country, wrote that his family was starting to feel the restrictions of rationing. Only bread, fruit, vegetables, wine, and tobacco were not rationed. The long, cold winter froze the potatoes in the cellar, but they were edible. In the near future, communications with the United States might be cut. The air on the Continent vibrated with rumors and lies, and it was nearly impossible to tell true from false information (Jung 1942c). In August, not long before mail from the U.S. to Switzerland was cut off, Jung told Esther Harding that Switzerland was like an island surrounded by abysmal darkness (Jung 1942d).

In early 1943, Allen Dulles, mission chief of the U.S. Office of Strategic Services in Switzerland during the War, reported to David Bruce, head of the OSS in London, about a view of Jung regarding Hitler. Mary Bancroft, a patient and friend of Jung and intimate friend of Dulles in Switzerland, had introduced him to Jung. Dulles told Bruce that Jung's opinion on Hitler, in view of the latter's psychopathic characteristics, should not be disregarded. Jung believed that Hitler would take recourse to any desperate measures to the end, including the possibility of suicide (Dulles 1943/1995). Jung's view proved to be correct. On Dulles and Jung, see Joan Dulles Buresch-Talley, "The C.G. Jung and Allen Dulles Correspondence," in Aryeh Maidenbaum, ed., *Jung and the Shadow of Anti-Semitism* (2002/2003) and Bair (2003), Ch. 31, "Agent 488."

Since mail from the U.S. to Switzerland had been cut off, Mary Mellon had been unable to write to Jung. In 1943, however, it became possible for letters to be carried in the diplomatic pouch of the Swiss courier, Adolph Haettenschwiller. Mary resumed her correspondence by asking Jung to give her the English-language rights to his works (Mellon 1943). He, however, did not give her these rights at this time (see Schoenl 1998, pp. 26-27, 32). At Christmas time she sent Jung her holiday greetings, to which he replied that he was happy to receive them and that he was well (Jung 1944a).

During 1944, Jung fell ill and nearly died from emboli in the heart and lungs. Mary cabled him in June because she had heard he was ill and asked whether he was all right. She signed the telegram: "All love" (Mellon 1944a). He thanked her and responded that he was recovering from a serious illness. He had just returned from the hospital and was much better (Jung 1944b). Mary replied that she was so glad he was better, and expressed her best wishes for his full recovery. She again signed the telegram: "All love" (Mellon 1944b). A telegram for his birthday followed on 26 July: she hoped he was steadily improving, wished him happy birthday, and signed it: "All love" (Mellon 1944c).

The Western Allies invaded occupied France in June 1944. In November, Esther Harding wrote Jung that the mails from the U.S. to Switzerland were open for private letters. Due to a clause in the

U.S. international postal agreements no letters until now could pass through occupied France from the U.S. Thus they had been unable to communicate with Jung since autumn 1942 (Harding 1944).

Allegations in the United States in 1944 that Jung was pro-Nazi

The literature on Jung contains little on the attacks on him in the United States before World War II in Europe ended. We believe this *lacuna* in the literature exists because relevant primary sources have not been examined. With this in mind, we examined Jung's largely unpublished correspondences with Eleanor Bertine and Esther Harding, who informed him of the attacks.

Shortly after the mail service had been opened to Switzerland, Bertine wrote Jung in December 1944 that for some time various rumors had come to them accusing Jung of being pro-Nazi in an apparent attempt to discredit his work. Some weeks previously, a Federal Bureau of Investigation agent had interviewed Bertine to try to discover whether Jung was anti-Semitic and connected with the Nazis. To Bertine's question why a Swiss citizen's opinion might concern the FBI, the agent replied that an informant had given the FBI suspicious information including a statement that Jung was now in the United States. Bertine related a second recent incident to Jung. The suggestion that she be invited to give a few lectures at the New School for Social Research in New York City had been met with the allegation that Jung was pro-Nazi, and, therefore, they hesitated to participate in spreading his ideas. To date she had not been invited. She also reported a third recent incident to Jung: the *New Republic* on 4 December had published a review of A.A. Brill's *Freud's Contribution to Psychiatry* in which the reviewer, Fredric Wertham, a psychiatrist in New York City, irrelevantly averred that Jung had betrayed Freud's progressive viewpoint and had become an important influence on Fascist philosophy in Europe. To Bertine it looked like a deliberate smear campaign was being conducted (Bertine 1944).

A FBI investigation on Jung had begun after a telephone call from someone—name excised—saying that an internationally known figure—Jung—was pro-Nazi and was now in the United States. A FBI Special Agent made a report in New York City on 13 September 1944. In the copies of the FBI documents that we obtained by a Freedom of Information Act request, the FBI excised the names and any identifying information of sources from the report. Therefore, in what follows, we will refer to each as "a source". The details in the report contained much false hearsay! "A source" heard that Jung had "turned Nazi" and had become head of a college in Berlin and head of medical societies. He or she recently heard that Jung was presently in the U.S. "A source" heard that after Hitler came to power after 1936 [sic], Jung was called to Berlin and replaced Sigmund Freud as president of medical societies! The source said that unless Jung was 100% Nazi this would not have happened. But he had not heard that Jung was currently in the U.S. "A source" provided a description of Jung. The report noted that some persons who knew Jung would be interviewed in New York City regarding whether he was in the U.S. and whether his activities were pro-Nazi or anti-American (Schoenl 1998, pp. 33-35).

On 28 October 1944, a second FBI report was made in New York City. An interviewee stated that from a source he could not remember he learned that Jung seemed an admirer of Hitler, had separated himself from Freud's teachings, and had become a believer in intuition which Hitler exemplified. The interviewee could not say whether Jung had in any way assisted the Nazis, but, on the basis of Jung's philosophy and admiration for Hitler, he considered Jung undoubtedly the philosophical head of the Nazi movement in Switzerland! A second interviewee—a woman, perhaps Eleanor Bertine or Esther Harding—stated that allegations that Jung was an admirer of Hitler, pro-German, or anti-Semitic were ridiculous. Apparently the same interviewee noted further that, since Jung had broken from and attacked Freud's theories, he created enmity from some Freudians. Jung had psychoanalyzed some persons in history, noting good and bad points. Since he had used Hitler as an example of some of his theories, some Freudians—misinterpreting his findings—might have branded him pro-German and anti-Semitic. Another interviewee also emphatically stated that Jung was neither pro-Nazi nor anti-Semitic. In view of the fact that Jung was not in the U.S. and all interviewed affirmed that he remained in Switzerland, the case was closed (Schoenl 1998, pp. 35-36).

On 10 January 1945, Charles Baudouin, a professor at the University of Geneva, talked with Jung in Kuesnacht. Jung spoke of the possession rampant in Nazi Germany. He added that some Germans met secretly at night and prayed for deliverance from "the Antichrist" (Baudouin 1945, pp. 147-48).

After the victory in the Battle of the Bulge in the winter, the Western Allies closed in on Germany from the West as the Soviets were closing in from the East. They crossed the Rhine, the last natural obstacle, in March. The end of the war in Europe was now in sight. On 23 April 1945, Jung wrote to Harding he had heard that day that Allied forces had reached Lake Constance. The Swiss were freed from the "murderous swarms of German beasts" surrounding them. Only Switzerland's eastern frontier remained "in touch with the devils" (Jung 1945a). He remarked that Bertine seemed worried by the ridiculous rumors that he was a Nazi. He further commented that he was on the black list of the Nazis and, had they moved into Switzerland, he would long ago have been shot. He suggested that the reason he had become President of the General Medical Society for Psychotherapy in 1933 and editor of its journal was that the German psychotherapists were threatened with extinction by the Nazi regime. For this reason he had asked Dr. Matthias H. Goering, a cousin of "the fat swine, the Marshall [Hermann Goering]," to be co-editor. But Jung said he soon discovered the whole Nazism was making for hell (Jung 1945a). We think Jung would have served Harding and Bertine better in defending him had he acknowledged that—although he was not pro-Nazi—besides the noble reason of saving psychotherapy in Germany from extinction, another reason existed in the shadow for his actions. We agree with Aryeh Maidenbaum, and we provided evidence in Chapter 1, that this reason was to advance Jungian psychology—his psychology—in Germany and elsewhere.

The end of the war and Jung's views in 1945

Hitler committed suicide on 30 April 1945 as Soviet forces were taking Berlin. Three days after Germany's formal surrender on 8 May, an interview of Jung by Peter Schmid was published in *Die Weltwoche* (Zurich). In "Wotan" in March 1936 Jung had suggested that Germans should not be judged so much as responsible agents but perhaps regarded also as victims of what was happening in their country (Jung 1936a/1970, para. 398). In striking contrast, now after World War II in Europe, he said that for the psychologist the question of collective guilt was a fact and to get the Germans to admit this guilt would be a most important task of therapy. He commented that, under Nazism, the demons got human beings into their power and inflated them into lunatic "supermen"—first, Hitler who then infected the rest. Every Nazi leader was possessed (Jung 1945b, pp. 150, 152). A similarity to Jung's "Wotan" essay was that he again said that Hitler was possessed and then possessed others. We point out that in this interview in May 1945, however, Jung did not mention the Wotan archetype. He seems now to have sensed that it was an inadequate explanation for what had happened in Germany.

Jung elaborated on German collective guilt in a 25 May letter to a German author, Herman Ullmann, as well as in an article, "After the Catastrophe," in June. To Ullmann, he said that Schmid had included in the interview in *Die Weltwoche* only what he understood and left out some important conditional or parenthetical comments. The concept of collective guilt thus remained hanging in mid-air. Germany's collective guilt consisted in the fact that Germans undoubtedly started the war and committed the atrocities of the concentration camps. Since they were Germans and these things occurred within the German frontier, all Germans were befouled. Further, since they happened in Europe, all Europeans were besmirched. German collective guilt was a psychological fact, not a moral or judicial construction. It was important that Germans should admit their guilt and not just foist it on others. The individual German could not shake off this obligation simply by blaming others, for example, the wicked Nazis (Jung 1973, pp. 369-70).

In June, Jung further elaborated on his concept of psychological collective guilt and gave its thrust in the first paragraphs of his article, "After the Catastrophe" (1945c/1970). He began by saying for the first time since 1936 when he published "Wotan" (1936a/1970) Germany's fate drove him to take up his pen. The psychological concept of collective guilt was painfully wide in scope. It was not, however, guilt in a legal or moral sense. The world saw Europe as the continent where the concentration camps grew, even as Europe singled out Germany as the country and people enveloped in a cloud of guilt. The horror occurred in Germany, and Germans were its perpetrators—which no German could deny. Germans could not rid themselves of collective guilt by protesting that they did not know. Psychological collective guilt hit Germany as the place where the horrible thing occurred. It was like a dark cloud enveloping the scene of a crime (Jung 1945c/1970, paras. 400, 402-405, 407).

Later in the piece, Jung stated that his observations of Hitler led him to conclude in 1937 that the final catastrophe would be far bloodier than he had previously supposed, for this "theatrical hysteric" now had the armored divisions of the army and German heavy industry's weight behind him. Jung implicitly said that his own view of Nazi Germany had been different in 1933-34 when he stated that our judgment would be different had our knowledge stopped short at 1933 or 1934. He went on to say that then, in Germany as well as Italy, some things seemed plausible and in favor of the regime, for example, unemployment declined. Europe looked on, prepared at most for a heavy shower (Jung 1945c/1970, paras. 419-420). Here Jung had the opportunity to acknowledge more clearly and openly that his view of Nazi Germany had been different from 1933 to February 1934, but he did not. Had he openly acknowledged this, he might have served his defenders better. We saw and acknowledged in Chapter 1 that his views of the Nazis and of statements that might seem anti-Semitic somewhat changed after Nazi Germany's first year. In spring 1934, he became warier of the Nazis. Subsequently, from 1934 on, he became increasingly warier of them (see Chapters 1-2).

Toward the end of July, Bertine wrote Jung that the New School for Social Research had at last ventured to have three lectures on Jungian psychology by Frances Wickes, Violet de Laszlo, and her—three prominent Jungian psychologists in New York City. She took the opportunity in her lecture to note the utter incompatibility of Jung's viewpoint with any collective "ism." She thought the attacks on Jung seemed to have blown over (Bertine 1945a). But they had not.

Though Bertine and colleagues were permitted to give a few lectures on Jungian psychology at the New School for Social Research, Jung's psychological ideas were unwelcome in Academia in psychology departments for many, many years. The historical significance of the World War II attacks on Jung is that they were the foreshadowing of the attacks on Jung to come in the United States.

In a letter to Mary Mellon on 24 September 1945, Jung responded to the allegations in the U.S. that he was a Nazi sympathizer. He stated that he had been on the Gestapo's black list and would have been on the spot had Germany invaded Switzerland (Jung

1945e). He told Mary that his students in Germany had to repudiate his views publicly. He said that "Freudian Jews" in the U.S. had started the rumor that he was a Nazi. The rumor he was a Nazi had been spread over the world. Then, with unfortunate words, he angrily went on. He said "the anti-christianism of the Jews" was difficult to mention after the horrible things that occurred in Germany. He remarked that Jews were not "so damned innocent after all," that intellectual Jews' role in pre-war Germany would be interesting to examine. Here he seems to have in mind his view that the materialism of some intellectuals, including Freud, had contributed to a religious vacuum in pre-war Germany into which Nazism moved. For example, in a letter to Dr. B. Cohen on 26 March 1934, Jung said that he opposed Freud and criticized him because of his materialistic, in-tellectualistic, and, not least, irreligious attitude, but not because he was Jewish (Jung 1973, p. 154; Maidenbaum 2002/2003, pp. 233-34). Then, returning to the allegation that he was a Nazi, he told Mary that already in 1934 he had challenged the Nazis at a reception in Baron von Schnitzler's house in Frankfurt. He had told them their counterclockwise Swastika was whirling down into unconsciousness and evil (Jung 1945e). Thus he denied that he had ever been a Nazi.

To Eugen Kolb, the Geneva correspondent of *Mishmar* of Tel Aviv, who wrote Jung on 4 September 1945 to ask questions on Hitler, Jung responded on 14 September. To the question, how did he as a psychiatrist view Hitler, he answered that he viewed Hitler primarily as an hysteric, in particular, *pseudologia phantastica*, a pathological liar. Such people might use any means to realize their wish fantasies and attain their aim. They might believe they did it for the benefit of the nation and did not see that their aim was egoistic. To the question were Hitler's contemporaries who executed his plans also psychopathic, Jung answered that suggestion worked only when a secret wish existed to fulfill it. Hitler worked on those who compensated their inferiority complex with dreams of power and social aspirations. Hitler collected an army of psychopaths, social misfits, and criminals around him. But he also gripped the unconscious of normal people. Jung's letter in answer to Kolb's questions went unpublished until 15 November 1974, in *Mishmar* (Jung 1945d/1976, paras. 1384, 1386, and n.1).

In 1945, Jung hoped that allegations that he was a Nazi sympathizer might blow over; however, that did not happen. They were repeated many times privately and publicly in the following years—even into the twenty-first century (for example, see Boynton 2004, p. A8; Friedman 2004, p. 2; Carvajal 2005, pp. E1, 6; Kaplan 2005, p. A14). As we have seen in Chapters 2-3 of the present book, Jung was definitely not a Nazi sympathizer even as his views on Nazi Germany evolved from 1934 to the end of World War II in 1945. We hope that this book will contribute to a resolution of the issue.

Chapter 4
Epilogue: Post-War Attacks on Jung: 1945-1946

The historical significance of the post-World War II attacks on Jung alleging that he was pro-Nazi and anti-Semitic, in addition to the earlier attacks during the war, is that they foreshadowed the attacks to come on him in the next seventy years, especially in the United States. In September 1945 an article entitled "Dr. C.G. Jung and National Socialism" by S.S. Feldman, M.D., appeared in the *American Journal of Psychiatry*—official organ of the American Psychiatric Association. In it Feldman suggested that Jung had been anti-Semitic and that Jung became anti-Nazi only after World War II in Europe ended. After saying that Jung had accused Freud and Alfred Adler of starting a negative psychology because they as Jews could see only faults and not virtues, Feldman translated some controversial statements in Jung's article "On the Present State of Psychotherapy," in the *Zentralblatt fuer Psychotherapy* in February 1934: "The young Germanic race is still able to create new forms of culture…. The Jew, as relatively a nomad, has never had and never will have, his own culture…. The Aryan unconscious has a higher potential than the Jewish, and this is the advantage and also the disadvantage of a young people close to the barbarian." Freud "and his Germanic followers could not

51

understand the German psyche. Have they been taught a better lesson by the powerful National-socialism at which the whole world looks with admiration—a movement which pervades a whole people and is manifest in every German individual?" (Feldman 1945). In contrast to these statements, Feldman cited Jung's interview in *Die Weltwoche* on Victory in Europe Day in 1945: "Today, the German resembles a drunkard awakening with a hangover, not knowing or not willing to know what he had done. He will try frantically to rehabilitate himself in the face of the world's accusations and hate—but that is not the right way. The only right way is his unconditional acknowledgment of guilt." (Feldman 1945).

On 18 November, James Kirsch wrote Jung that he was hearing again and again the rumor that Jung was a Nazi. Kirsch said that in each case he had been able to trace it to a Freudian and that it fit well into the Freudian attempt to be regarded as the only form of depth psychology. A whispering campaign was hard to fight. He cited Feldman's article in the *American Journal of Psychiatry* (Kirsch 1945).

On 24 November, Harding wrote Jung also informing him that slanderous rumors concerning his supposed relation to Nazism were again cropping up in the United States. She told him that Bertine was busy writing an article in refutation of Feldman's article. Harding suggested that a group of interested persons keep repeating and spreading the rumors, for left to themselves they would have died a natural death (Harding 1945a).

Shortly thereafter, Bertine wrote to Jung. She said that the rumors about Jung being pro-Nazi were now circulating with renewed venom. Having only recently learned of Feldman's article, she and Harding were writing an answer for possible submission to the *American Journal of Psychiatry* and enclosed a copy for Jung's consideration. Of more immediate concern, however, was another attack just published in the *New York Herald Tribune*, one of the largest newspapers in the U.S., on 2 December. Albert D. Parelhoff, its author, subsequently became Jung's most persistent attacker. The attack seemed part of a campaign to keep Jung from getting into circulation, as Parelhoff had told Geoffrey Parsons, the *Tribune's* editor (Bertine 1945b). In a 21 December 1945 letter to Allen Dulles, Parsons said that while the campaign against Jung was in full cry, its leaders had little to go on, and he did not want to keep giving them space (Buresch-Talley 2002/2003. p. 46).

In his attack in the *Tribune* on 2 December, Parelhoff charged that Jung was pro-Nazi in his views and actions. Citing Feldman's article, Parelhoff said it also exposed Jung's anti-Semitism and Jung's attempted reversal of position when *Die Weltwoche*, a leading Swiss weekly, interviewed him on Victory in Europe Day. Parelhoff cited in contrast H.R. Knickerbocker's interview of Jung, "Diagnosing the Dictators," published in *Cosmopolitan Magazine*, January 1939. Parelhoff claimed that in it Jung was prolific with Nazi-Fascist statements such as: "I couldn't help liking Mussolini. His bodily energy and elasticity are warm, human and contagious," and "there was in his [Hitler's] eyes the look of a seer. There is no question that Hitler belongs in the category of the truly mystic medicine man." Parelhoff said that Jung's advice to the Western democracies then was: "Instinct should tell the Western statesmen not to touch Germany in her present mood. She is much too dangerous.... So I say studying Germany as I would a patient, and

Europe as I would a patient's family and neighbors, let her go into Russia. There is plenty of land there" (Parelhoff 1945, 2 December).

In their reply to Parelhoff's attack, Bertine and Harding stated that they knew Jung well personally and professionally for 25 years, discussed Nazism with him in 1933, '35, '36, and '37, and received many unequivocal letters since then. To show that he had been strongly opposed to Nazism's tenets, they cited his Terry lectures at Yale University in 1937, published as *Psychology and Religion* in 1938, and from his paper "Psychotherapy in our time" in 1941. To Parelhoff's suggestion that Jung admired Hitler when he spoke of him as a seer and mystic in the *Cosmopolitan* interview in January 1939, Bertine and Harding replied that in discussing the differences between the dictators, Jung spoke of Hitler as a seer and mystic because of his hunches, intuition, and dependence on his unconscious voices. Hitler was an interesting study to the psychologist but untrustworthy as a leader. In addition, they noted that the Nazis placed Jung's name on their black list. They pointed out that Jung had a following in the United States that included a number of refugees from Germany. They said any of these would corroborate the facts stated in this letter. They concluded that, in contrast to Nazism, Jung's life work was dedicated to freeing the individual from the tyranny of the collective, whether manifested as a mass prejudice or the state's overgrown power (Bertine & Harding 1945, 9 December).

In a letter of the same date, Bertine informed Jung that she and Harding were writing a second and stronger draft of an answer to Feldman's attack in the *American Journal of Psychiatry*. She enclosed their letter published in the *New York Herald Tribune* in reply to Parelhoff's attack there. She admitted that the answer was "pretty bob-tailed." Limitation of space had precluded a fuller answer in the *Tribune* (Bertine 1945c).

An undated letter by Bertine to Jung later in December, however, introduced new considerations. She suggested that to do nothing at all save sit tight and wait might be wiser than to answer the attack in the *American Journal of Psychiatry*. She remarked that the wolves were really out for blood this time. To explain Jung's viewpoint in the 1930s, she and Harding would have to show that he was differing from the reductive methods of Freudian analysis and not from Jews. This would stir up vocal hatred of Freudians, who, she thought, intuit that Jung undermines their basis of security. Whatever she and Harding would write would thus arouse renewed passionate resentment. Moreover, vis-à-vis Jungians, Freudians were in the enormous majority among psychiatrists in the U.S., and Bertine and Harding feared they might only stir up a worse stink by answering Feldman's attack in the *American Journal of Psychiatry* (Bertine 1945d).

Furthermore, in this letter by Bertine, their need for a closer understanding with Jung came up regarding their answer in the *New York Herald Tribune*. Jung had said he was on the Nazis' black list, so, taking him literally, Bertine and Harding had made that statement in their letter to the *Tribune*. Subsequently Fredric Wertham, a psychiatrist in New York City and President of the Society for the Advancement of Psychotherapy, wrote the *Tribune* a "typically Freudian letter" referring to their unconscious motives, flatly contradicting their statement, and saying he had a copy of the black list. Bertine commented this ought not happen— suggesting her and Harding's need to be on the same wavelength as Jung to answer effectively (Bertine 1945d). Many years later,

Bair (2003) provided some evidence that Jung had been on the *Schwarze Liste* (Black List) of authors whose works were banned in Germany (Bair 2003, pp. 462, 800). Bertine's feeling at the time, however, was that she and Harding should stir up no more hornets (Bertine 1945d). Thus they did not answer Feldman in the *American Journal of Psychiatry*.

We have examined the two drafts of their unpublished answer in the Jung Archives, Swiss Federal Institute of Technology, Zurich. In their drafts they say that Jung accepted the presidency of the General Medical Society for Psychotherapy in 1933 and editorship of its *Zentralblatt* to keep the lamp of psychotherapy burning—as he told one of them in 1935 (probably Bertine who saw him in Switzerland that year). We think they could have written a stronger answer had Jung acknowledged that, besides this noble reason, a reason in the shadow also existed: to promote his psychology in Germany and elsewhere. In both drafts of their answer Bertine and Harding discuss Feldman's purported translation from Jung's article in the *Zentralblatt*, Vol. 7 (1934), and, in particular, the words: "Have they been taught a better lesson by the powerful National Socialism at which the whole world looks with admiration?" In their first draft, they say the sentence was tampered with in Germany before publication, and the phrase "at which the whole world looks with admiration" was interpolated. In the revised draft, they rightly regard the words as Feldman's mistranslation. Their translation is: "Has the mighty apparition of National Socialism, which the whole world views with astounded eyes, taught them better?" (Bertine & Harding 1945, December). The translation in *The Collected Works of C.G. Jung* is similar: "Has the formidable phenomenon of National Socialism, on which the whole world gazes with astonished eyes, taught them better?" (*CW* 10, 354). In his article, Feldman suggested that Jung became anti-Nazi only after World War II in Europe ended. In the replies in their drafts, Bertine and Harding persuasively cite Jung's words in letters to them. In September 1939, after Nazi Germany invaded Poland, Jung remarked that the conviction existed in Switzerland that Germany had to an unspeakable degree lost its national honor. In February 1940, while the war was quiet during the winter, he commented it was appalling to see how Germany's cultural level was rapidly sinking because of the complete suffocation of free thought. He further commented that Nazi Germany's treatment of Poland and Czechoslovakia showed everybody around Germany what was in store if it won the war. In August 1942, he wrote that Switzerland was like an island surrounded by the surging tide of abysmal "tenebrosity" (darkness). Subsequently mail communication with Switzerland was interrupted; in November 1944, as we have seen, Bertine and Harding resumed their correspondence with Jung. In the first draft, they cited as further evidence Jung's letter to Harding of 23 April 1945 in which he said that the Swiss were now liberated from the nightmare of "the murderous swarms of the German beasts" surrounding them on all sides. Thus in their drafts of an answer Bertine and Harding demonstrated that Jung was anti-Nazi during World War II, and they refuted Feldman's suggestion that Jung became anti-Nazi only after the end of the war in Europe (Bertine & Harding 1945, December). But they had not demonstrated that in the early 1930s Jung had been in no degree anti-Semitic nor that he had no sympathy with the Nazis then. Thus their answer would have, at best, only partially succeeded.

On 23 December 1945, Bertine wrote Dr. Elizabeth Whitney, a Jungian analyst in the San Francisco area, to update her and, through her, Jungians on the West Coast on Bertine's and Harding's drafts of an answer. Jung had just sent Bertine a brief message saying please do nothing presently. She thought this might be the wisest course and remarked that evidence got nowhere against impassioned vituperation except to anger it further (Bertine 1945e). On December 23 and 29, Harding also wrote Whitney concluding that just to let the issue lie might be best, though to hear Jung maligned made her boil (Harding 1945b). They thought the attacks on Jung might blow over. Allegations that Jung was a Nazi sympathizer and anti-Semitic, however, did not blow over.

In January 1946, the *American Journal of Psychiatry* published a letter to the editor by Dr. Gotthard Booth, M.D., and a rejoinder by Feldman. Booth pointed out that Feldman's article had misrepresented Jung as having been an admirer of Nazism who allegedly changed his view on V-E day and that this impression was created partly by arbitrary quotation. Feldman had mistranslated Jung's German text to read: "National-Socialism at which the whole world looks *with admiration*" instead of the correct translation "*with astonished eyes.*" Furthermore, Jung's concept of a basic psychological difference between the Jewish and the German mind never included the Nazi distinction between inferior race and master race (Booth 1946, p. 555). In reply, Feldman maintained "admiration" most adequately expressed the spirit of the text. However, allowing that Booth might be right in saying that the correct translation was "with astonished eyes," Feldman did "not feel that it changes the sentiment expressed by Jung" (Feldman 1946, p. 555).

Epilogue: Post-War Attacks on Jung: 1945-1946

Subsequently the *American Journal of Psychiatry* received a letter from Gerhard Adler, one of Jung's oldest pupils who was a Jewish refugee from Germany to Great Britain, and a letter from Ernest Harms, another pupil of Jung, calling attention to inaccuracies in Feldman's article. The *Journal* published its edited excerpts from these two letters in a piece titled "Dr. C.G. Jung and National Socialism." Adler expressed indebtedness to Jung for help to him and other Jews. He wrote: "It certainly seems rather absurd to accuse Jung of antisemitism or sympathy with National Socialism when so many of his pupils have been Jews; and none of them has ever found the slightest reason to accuse Jung of antisemitism or of being a Nazi." Adler noted "the egregious mistranslation"—"admiration" rather than "amazement" or "astonishment"—to which Booth's letter had already referred. Adler further commented that Feldman had inaccurately translated "*Kulturform*" as "culture." Jung had written that the Jew has never had "his own cultural form ('Kulturform')." Adler remarked: "Dr. Feldman seems unable to grasp the difference between 'culture' and 'cultural form' ('Kultur' and 'Kulturform')." Further on in his letter, Adler pointed out that one can hold different opinions from Jung regarding Jewish psychology and Jung's interpretation of it, but they need "to be discussed on the psychological and not on the political level. Dr. Feldman's article is nothing but a repetition of the Freudian attempt to discredit Jung's psychological views by discrediting his political views." Regarding Jung's attitude toward Nazism, Adler cited Jung's 1937 Terry Lectures on "Psychology and Religion" at Yale University (published in 1938): "Now we behold the amazing spectacle of states taking over the age-old claim of theocracy, that is, of totality, inevitably accompanied by

59

suppression of free opinion…trying to create a state slavery and a state prison devoid of any mental or spiritual charm." Adler concluded that Feldman's article created by mistranslation and misrepresentation a wrong and unfair picture of Jung ([Correspondences] 1946, pp. 702-3).

In his letter, Harms commented that Jung accepted the presidency of the General Medical Society for Psychotherapy (GMSP) and editorship of its *Zentralblatt* in 1933 "to preserve international cooperation and assist those amongst his colleagues who were tied down in Germany." Harms remarked that Feldman wanted to represent Jung as anti-Semitic. Harms observed that it "would take a long article to explain the real facts of the relationship between Sigmund Freud and C.G. Jung, which have, of course, not been the happiest." In contrast to anti-Semitism Harms then referred to Jung's address at the Convention of the International GMSP in May 1934 in which Jung paid tribute to Freud, for which Jung was "berated by the Nazi press" ([Correspondences] 1946, pp. 702-3).

Despite the points that Adler and Harms made, their letters in the *American Journal of Psychiatry* nevertheless had a significant weakness. They did not address the possibility that Jung's views of the Nazis and of statements that might seem anti-Semitic evolved over time and, in particular, that his views during Nazi Germany's first year (from 30 January 1933 to February 1934: see Chapter 1) were somewhat different from his views thereafter. Harms' letter had a second weakness. Though he correctly said that Jung accepted the presidency of the GMSP and editorship of its *Zentralblatt* in 1933 to preserve the international connection among psychotherapists and to assist colleagues in Germany where psychotherapy was threatened, his letter did not recognize the possibility of an additional reason in the shadow: to advance Jungian psychology in Germany and elsewhere (see Chapter 1).

Parelhoff became Jung's most persistent attacker. In June-July 1946 he began a series of articles falsely alleging that Jung was a Nazi collaborationist—"Dr. Carl G. Jung—Nazi Collaborationist." In the first article he said that the so-called way of healing of Jung "openly merged with the Heil Hitler! *weg* [way] of the Nazis" in the latter part of 1933. Parelhoff asserted that after Hitler was in unquestionable control in Germany, Jung threw all caution to the winds and became a Nazi collaborationist; in Jung's editorial in the *Zentralblatt fuer Psychotherapie* in December 1933 he laid down the new policy of the journal, "which will differentiate between the 'Germanic' and 'Jewish' psychologies." A communication from Matthias H. Goering, the leader of the reorganized German section of the General Medical Society for Psychotherapy followed that declared its members should make a serious study of Hitler's *Mein Kampf* and recognize it as a basic work. Parelhoff went on to say that Jung had allied himself with an "organization of sadistic degenerates and murderers" and that the Nazi plan called for attacks on Jews in all fields. Jung then wasted no time, Parelhoff asserted, in establishing himself as a Nazi collaborationist. In the next issue of the *Zentralblatt* in his article "The Present State of Psychotherapy," Jung made these statements: "The Jews have this peculiarity in common with women: being physically weaker, they must aim at the breaches in the armor of their adversary.... The Jew, as a relative nomad, never has had and never will have his own culture, for his instincts and his abilities necessitate his living among a more or less cultured host.... The Aryan unconscious has a higher potential than the Jewish." Parelhoff concluded that the "healing way" of Jung had merged with the Heil Hitler! way of the Nazis (Parelhoff 1946a, pp. 22, 26-28).

Parelhoff's second article appeared in the next issue. He said that in Jung's reply to Gustav Bally in the *Neue Zuercher Zeitung* in March 1934 Jung emphasized the altruistic motives for coming to the rescue of his German colleagues; Parelhoff, however, wrongly alleged that Jung confessed that it was necessary, since the *Zentralblatt* was published in Germany, for all its associates to pledge allegiance and politically to be above reproach. Parelhoff went on again to say that Jung voluntarily collaborated with the Nazis. He criticized Harvard University's conferral of an honorary doctorate upon Jung in 1936. He added that more honors were to come. Yale University would invite him to deliver the Terry Lectures in 1937 and Oxford University would confer upon him an honorary degree in 1938. Parelhoff remarked: "It was only natural that he was to grow increasingly confident of total victory for Hitler and the Nazis and, accordingly, that he was to become bolder and more arrogant." In conclusion, Parelhoff said that additional findings had necessitated a third article by him, and it would appear in the next issue (Parelhoff 1946b, pp. 26-29, 31.)

Although Parelhoff is an extreme example, his articles illustrate that if one starts with the mold that Jung was a Nazi collaborationist and anti-Semitic one may force some passages from Jung into that mold. Parelhoff's articles were not scholarly. In a visit to Karl Shapiro at Johns Hopkins University, he referred to himself as "a private individual in commerce" (Shapiro 1949).

The third and last in his series of articles appeared in February-March 1947. Here Parelhoff cited a passage in Jung's essay "Wotan" in 1936 that Wotan would not exhibit restless, stormy, and violent qualities only but might display other aspects in the future and that if "this be true, National Socialism will not be the last word. In the next few years or *decades* [italics Parelhoff's], we may look for things that as yet lie in the background, whose nature we are not yet able to conceive." But Jung was expressing here a possible future hope for Germany, not for Nazism. Parelhoff wrongly interpreted it as Jung expressing confidence in ultimate, lasting victory for Nazism and that Wotan and the Nazis, after decades, might achieve a gentler mood. He went on to say that by autumn 1937 the method of Jung's pro-Nazi propaganda should have been clear to rational people: it was to use propaganda that was most effective for the occasion. Parelhoff reminded the reader that in 1937 Yale University bestowed on Jung the honor of delivering the Terry Lectures. In 1938 Oxford University bestowed an honorary degree on him. By the end of 1938 Jung was, Parelhoff remarked, "supremely confident of the ultimate, complete victory of Nazism." In January 1939 Jung's interview by H.R. Knickerbocker appeared in Hearst's *Cosmopolitan*. Parelhoff called it a "blatant piece of pro-Nazi propaganda." He said that in it "Jung continued to expound on the supernatural, god-like powers of Hitler" and that Jung warred for Hitler and Nazism with his "scientific" psychological weapons when he said that Hitler had a twofold secret: his unconscious had exceptional access to his conscious and he let himself be moved by it. He was like a man who listened to a stream of suggestions from a mysterious source and then acted on them. Later in 1939, Jung's book *The Integration of the Personality* was published by Farrar & Rinehart (Jung 1939e). Parelhoff said that Jung declared (pp. 272-

73) regarding the God whom Nietzsche said was dead, that "*it may be that he has come back again in the disguise of the 'superhuman'*" [italics Parelhoff's]. Then Parelhoff erroneously attempted to connect this to previous writings of Jung. In his editorial in the *Zentralblatt* in December 1933 Jung wrote of "the definite differences between 'Germanic' and 'Jewish' psychology." Beginning with his essay "Wotan" in March 1936, Parelhoff asserted, Jung advocated the worship of Wotan for the Germans. Now, in 1939, Parelhoff wrongly alleged, the God Jung extolled was the one who has "come back again in the disguise of the 'superhuman,'" namely, Adolf Hitler. Parelhoff went on to say that after World War II began Jung adopted the policy of silence in public on Nazism and that nothing further was heard of him on the subject until V-E Day in May 1945 when *Die Weltwoche,* a leading Swiss weekly, published an interview with him. Parelhoff commented that with the defeat of Nazi Germany and the death of Hitler, "the ever-expedient" Jung stated that the German today resembled a drunkard awakening with a hangover and not knowing or willing to know what he had done. In the face of the world's accusations, he would frantically try to rehabilitate himself, but that was "not the right way. The only right way is his unconditional acknowledgment of guilt." Parelhoff remarked: "First of the Nazi collaborationists to turn about and attack Germany was Dr. Carl G. Jung. Now every German was guilty. But what of Dr. Jung himself?" Parelhoff said that to date Jung had not expressed one word of contrition regarding his aid to the Nazis. He added that here in the United States Jungians, to a person, "have determinedly denied Jung's guilt" (Parelhoff 1947, pp. 21-22, 24-26, 28-30).

Epilogue: Post-War Attacks on Jung: 1945-1946

For all their differences, Jung's postwar attackers and defenders had one thing in common. They did not recognize that Jung's views of the Nazis and of statements that seem anti-Semitic changed after 1933, Nazi Germany's first year (see Chapter 1), and that his views of Nazi Germany evolved during the following years (see Chapters 2-3). The allegations of the postwar attackers of Jung were largely false. Nevertheless, he would have served his defenders better had he openly acknowledged that his views had evolved.

References

Bair, D. (2003). *Jung: A biography*. Boston: Little, Brown.

Bally, G. (1934). "Deutschstaemmige Psychotherapie?" ("German-born psychotherapy?"). *Neue Zuercher Zeitung*, 343, 27 February 1934, 2.

Barrett, W. G. (1969). Unpublished interview with Gene F. Nameche, 1 May 1969. C.G. Jung Biographical Archive, Harvard Countway Library of Medicine, Boston, MA.

Baudouin, C. (1945/1977). From Charles Baudouin's journal, 10 January 1945. In *C.G. Jung speaking: Interviews and encounters*, eds. William McGuire and R. F. C. Hull. Princeton, NJ: Princeton University Press.

Bertine, E. (1944). "Bertine to Jung, 10 December 1944." Jung Archives, Swiss Federal Institute of Technology, Zurich (hereafter abbreviated JA Zurich).

Bertine, E. (1945a). "Bertine to Jung, 30 July 1945." JA Zurich.

Bertine, E. (1945b). "Bertine to Jung, 2 December 1945." JA Zurich.

Bertine, E. (1945c). "Bertine to Jung, 9 December 1945." JA Zurich.

Bertine, E. (1945d). "Bertine to Jung, [no date] December 1945." JA Zurich.

Bertine, E. (1945e). "Bertine to Elizabeth G. Whitney, 23 December 1945." Virginia Allan Detloff Library, C. G. Jung Institute of San Francisco, CA.

Bertine, E., & Harding, M. E. [Esther]. (1945, 9 December). "Letter to the editor." *New York Herald Tribune*, Section II, p. 7.

Bertine, E., & Harding, M. E. (1945, December), An answer to Dr. Feldman's article in *American Journal of Psychiatry*, September 1945, entitled Dr. Jung and National Socialism. Unpublished manuscript, two drafts. JA Zurich.

Booth, G. (1946). "Letter to the editor." *American Journal of Psychiatry*, 102 (January), 555.

Boynton, R. S. (2004, 11 January). "In the Jung Archives: Review of Bair's *Jung: A Biography*." *The New York Times*, p. A8.

Buresch-Talley, J. Dulles. (2002/2003). "The C.G. Jung and Allen Dulles correspondence." In A. Maidenbaum (Ed.), *Jung and the shadow of anti-Semitism*. Berwick, ME: Nicolas-Hays.

Carvajal, D. (2005, 3 August). "In Germany, Jung biography includes family denial." *The New York Times*, pp. E1, 6.

Churchill, W. (1937/1942). *Great contemporaries*. London: Macmillan.

[Correspondences]. (1946). "Dr. C.G. Jung and National Socialism." *American Journal of Psychiatry*, 102 (March), 702-3.

References

Dohe, C.B. (2016). Jung's wandering archetype: Race and religion in analytical psychology. London & New York: Routledge.

Dulles, A. (1943/1995). "Telegram from Dulles to Bruce, 3 February 1943." In J. Heideking & C. Mauch (Eds.), *American intelligence and the German resistance to Hitler*. Boulder, CO: Westview Press.

Federal Bureau of Investigation. (1944, September 13). "Unpublished report titled 'Dr. Carl G. Jung.'"

Federal Bureau of Investigation. (1944, October 28). "Unpublished report titled 'Dr. Carl G. Jung.'"

Feldman, S.S. (1945). "Dr. C.G. Jung and National Socialism." *American Journal of Psychiatry,* 102 (September), 263.

Feldman, S.S. (1946). "Letter to the editor." *American Journal of Psychiatry*, 102 (January), 555.

Friedman, H.J. (2004, 8 February). "Jung's anti-Semitism, letter to the editor." *The New York Times*, p. 2.

Frosh, S. (2005). "Jung and the Nazis: Some implications for psychoanalysis." *Psychoanalysis and History*, 7(2), 253-71.

Gilman, S.L. (1993). *Freud, race, and gender*. Princeton, NJ: Princeton University Press.

Harding, E. (1933-36). "Unpublished notebooks." C.G. Jung Foundation for Analytical Psychology, New York.

Harding, E. (1944). "Harding to Jung, 19 November 1944." JA Zurich.

Harding, E. (1945a). "Harding to Jung, 24 November 1945." JA Zurich.

Harding, E. (1945b). "Harding to Elizabeth G. Whitney, 23 and 29 December 1945." Virginia Allan Detloff Library, C.G. Jung Institute of San Francisco, CA.

Henderson, J. (1933). "Henderson to Jung, 1 May 1933." JA Zurich.

Henderson, J. (1968). "Unpublished interview with Gene F. Nameche, 14 December 1968." C.G. Jung Biographical Archive, Harvard Countway Library of Medicine, Boston, MA.

Jaffe, A. (1975). "Transcript of BBC interview with Aniela Jaffe, Joseph Wheelwright, and others." *Carl Gustav Jung: 1875-1961*. Produced by Adrian Johnson. Compiled and presented by Ean Begg. Copy in the Joseph and Jane Hollister Wheelwright. Collection, Opus Archives, Pacifica Graduate Institute, Santa Barbara, CA.

Jung, C.G. (1933a). "Jung to Cimbal, 4 September 1933." cited in Sorge (2010). p. 138.

Jung, C.G. (1933b/1970). "Editorial" tr. from *Zentralblatt fuer Psychotherapie*, 6 (December 1933), 139-40. *Civilization in transition. Collected Works* (hereafter abbreviated *CW*) 10, paras. 1014-15.

Jung, C.G. (1933c). "Jung to Kranefeldt, 20 December 1933." Jung Archives, Swiss Federal Institute of Technology, Zurich (hereafter abbreviated JA Zurich).

Jung, C.G. (1933d). "Jung to Heyer, 20 December 1933." JA Zurich.

References

Jung, C.G. (1934a). "Jung to Kranefeldt, 9 February 1934." quoted in Ostow (1977), 337.

Jung, C.G. (1934b/1970). "The state of psychotherapy today." tr. *Zur gegenwaertigen Lage der Psychotherapie, Zentralblatt fuer Psychotherapie*, 7 (February 1934), 1-16. *Civilization in transition. CW* 10, paras. 333-70.

Jung, C.G. (1934c/1970). "A rejoinder to Dr. Bally." tr. from *Neue Zuercher Zeitung*, 13 and 14 March 1934, 1. *Civilization in transition. CW* 10, paras. 1016-34.

Jung, C.G. (1934d). "Jung to van der Hoop, 12 March 1934." JA Zurich.

Jung, C.G. (1934e). "Jung to Heyer, 20 April 1934." JA Zurich.

Jung, C.G. (1934f). "Ueber Komplextheorie." Lecture at the Bad Nauheim Congress, *Zentral blatt fuer Psychotherapie* 7, 141.

Jung, C.G. (1934g). "Jung to Kirsch, 26 May 1934." quoted in Lammers (2011). p. 47.

Jung, C.G. (1934h/1976). *The Visions Seminars, from the complete notes of Mary Foote*. Zurich: Spring Publications.

Jung, C.G. (1935a). "Problems of Swiss and European psychotherapy." *Schweitzerische Aerztezeitung* 26. Archives of the C. G. Jung Institute, San Francisco, CA.

Jung, C.G. (1935b/1988). *Nietzsche's Zarathustra: Notes of the seminar given in 1934-1939*, vol. 1. Princeton: Princeton University Press.

Jung, C.G. (1935c). "Jung to Kranefeldt, 12 March 1935." JA Zurich.

Jung, C.G. (1935d/1976). "The Tavistock Lectures." *The symbolic life. CW* 18, paras. 1-415.

Jung, C.G. (1936a/1970). "Wotan." tr. *Wotan, Neue Schweizer Rundschau*, Zurich, n.s., 3 (March, 1936), 657-69. *Civilization in transition. CW* 10, paras. 371-99.

Jung, C.G. (1936b/1976). "Psychology and National Problems." A lecture delivered at the Tavistock Clinic, London, 14 October 1936. *The symbolic life. CW* 18, paras. 1305-42.

Jung, C.G. (1937/1938). "The Terry Lectures 1937." published as *Psychology and religion.* New Haven, CT: Yale University Press, 1938; reprinted 1955.

Jung, C.G. (1938a). "Jung to Ruth Bailey, Fall 1938." JA Zurich.

Jung, C.G. (1938b/1977). "Diagnosing the dictators." Interview with H.R. Knickerbocker, October 1938, in *Hearst's International-Cosmopolitan*, January 1939. In *C.G. Jung speaking: Interviews and encounters*, eds. W. McGuire and R.F.C. Hull. Princeton, NJ: Princeton University Press.

Jung, C.G. (1939a/1977). "Jung diagnoses the dictators." Interview with H.L. Philp, April 1939, in *The Psychologist*, London, May 1939. In *C.G. Jung speaking: Interviews and encounters.*

Jung, C.G. (1939b/1976). "The symbolic life." A seminar talk, 5 April 1939, to the Guild of Pastoral Psychology, London. *The symbolic life. CW* 18, paras. 608-96.

References

Jung, C.G. (1939c). "Jung to Esther Harding, 28 September 1939." JA Zurich.

Jung, C.G. (1939d). "Jung to Esther Harding, 4 November 1939." JA Zurich.

Jung, C.G. (1939e). *The Integration of the Personality*. New York: Farrar & Rinehart.

Jung, C.G. (1940a). "Jung to Esther Harding, 26 February 1940." JA Zurich.

Jung, C.G. (1940b). "Jung to Mary Mellon, 19 June 1940." JA Zurich.

Jung, C.G. (1940c). "Jung to Mary Mellon, 21 August 1940." JA Zurich.

Jung, C.G. (1940d). "Jung to Mary Mellon, 12 October 1940." JA Zurich.

Jung, C.G. (1941). "Jung to Mary Mellon, 7 January 1941." JA Zurich.

Jung, C.G. (1942a). "Jung to Mary Mellon, 31 January 1942." JA Zurich.

Jung, C.G. (1942b). "Jung to Esther Harding, 10 April 1942." JA Zurich.

Jung, C.G. (1942c). Jung to Mary Mellon, 10 April 1942, JA Zurich.

Jung, C.G. (1942d). "Jung to Esther Harding, August 1942." Quoted in Bertine & Harding, unpublished manuscript. An answer to Dr. Feldman's article in *American Journal of*

Psychiatry, September 1945, entitled Dr. C. G. Jung and National Socialism, 5 pages, JA Zurich.

Jung, C.G. (1944a). "Jung to Mary Mellon, 3 January 1944." JA Zurich.

Jung, C.G. (1944b). "Jung to Mary Mellon, 27 June 1944." JA Zurich.

Jung, C.G. (1945a). "Jung to Esther Harding, 23 April 1945." JA Zurich.

Jung, C.G. (1945b/1977). "Interview with Peter Schmid." In *Die Weltwoche*, Zurich, 11 May 1945. In *C. G. Jung speaking: Interviews and encounters.*

Jung, C.G. (1945c/1970). "After the catastrophe." tr. *Nach der Katastrophe, Neue Schweizer Rundschau*, Zurich, n. s., 13 (June 1945), 67-88. *Civilization in transition. CW* 10, paras. 400-443.

Jung, C.G. (1945d/1976). "Answers to *Mishmar* on Adolf Hitler, 1945." *The symbolic life. CW* 18, paras. 1384-87.

Jung, C.G. (1945e). "Jung to Mary Mellon, 24 September 1945." JA Zurich.

Jung, C.G. (1973). *C.G. Jung letters*, Vol. 1: 1906-1950. Eds. G. Adler with A. Jaffe. Trans. R. F. C. Hull. Princeton, NJ: Princeton University Press.

Jung, C.G. (1977). *C.G. Jung speaking: Interviews and encounters.* Eds. William McGuire and R. F. C. Hull. Princeton: NJ: Princeton University Press.

References

Kaplan, J. (2005, 8 August). "Jung biography, letter to the editor." *The New York Times*, A14.

Kirsch, J. (1945). "Kirsch to Jung, 18 November 1945." Quoted in Lammers (2011). p. 102.

Lammers, A.C. (Ed.). (2011). *The Jung-Kirsch letters*. London & New York, Routledge.

Lammers, A.C. (2012a). "Professional relationships in dangerous times: C. G. Jung and the Society for Psychotherapy." *Journal of Analytical Psychology*, 57(1), 99-119.

Lammers, A.C. (2012b). "James Kirsch's defense of Jung: *Juedische Rundschau*, 1934." *Jung Journal: Culture & Psyche*, 6(4), 74-84.

Lewin, N.A. (2009). *Jung on war, politics and Nazi Germany: Exploring the theory of archetypes and the collective unconscious*. London: Karnac Books.

Liebscher, M. (Ed.). (2015). *Analytical psychology in exile: The correspondence of C.G. Jungand Erich Neumann*. Trans. H. McCartney. Princeton, NJ: Princeton University Press.

Maidenbaum, A. (Ed.). (2002/2003). *Jung and the shadow of anti-Semitism*. Berwick, ME: Nicolas-Hays.

Mellon, M. (1943). "Mellon to Jung, no date [1943]." JA Zurich.

Mellon, M. (1944a). "Mellon to Jung, 23 June 1944." JA Zurich.

Mellon, M. (1944b). "Mellon to Jung, 1 July 1944." JA Zurich.

Mellon, M. (1944c). "Mellon to Jung, 26 July 1944." JA Zurich.

Murray, H.A., Jr. (1936). Article in reply to the statement printed in the Harvard *Crimson*, copy in Jung archives, Virginia Allan Detloff Library, C. G. Jung Institute of San Francisco, CA.

Neumann, E. (1934). "Neumann to Jung, [undated] 1934." Quoted in Liebscher (2015), pp. 10-15.

Nietzsche, F. (1883-91/1995). *Thus spoke Zarathustra. Also sprach Zarathustra*, tr. Walter Kaufmann. New York: Modern Library.

Ostow, M. (1977). "Letter to the editor." *International review of psycho-analysis*, 4, 377.

Parelhoff, A.D. (1945, 2 December). "Letter to the editor." *New York Herald Tribune*, Section II, p. 7.

Parelhoff, A.D. (1946a). "Dr. Carl G. Jung—Nazi collaborationist." *The Protestant*, 7 (June-July), 22-28.

Parelhoff, A.D. (1946b). "Dr. Carl G. Jung—Nazi collaborationist." *The Protestant*, 7 (August-September), 26-31.

Parelhoff, A.D. (1947). "Dr. Carl G. Jung—Nazi collaborationist." *The Protestant*, 7 (February-March), 17-30.

Parsons, G. "Letter to Allen Dulles, 21 December 1945." In J. D. Buresch-Talley, "The C.G. Jung and Allen Dulles correspondence." In A. Maidenbaum (Ed.) (2002/2003), *Jung and the shadow of anti-Semitism* (45-46). Berwick, ME: Nicolas-Hays.

Rasche, J. (2007). "Trying to understand and excusing is not the same." Lecture for IPA/IAAPpanel "Freud and the Freudians, Jung and the Jungians, during the Thirties and the Nazi-

References

Regime" at the 45th International IPA Congress in Berlin, 25-28 July 2007.

Rasche, J. (2012). "C.G. Jung in the 1930s: Not to idealize, neither to diminish." *Jung Journal:Culture and Psyche,* 6(4), 54-73.

Samuels, A. (1993). *The political psyche.* London & New York: Routledge.

Schoenl, W. (1998). *C. G. Jung: His friendships with Mary Mellon and J. B. Priestley.* Wilmette, IL: Chiron Publications.

Schoenl, W. (2009). "The World War II attacks on Jung: Eleanor Bertine's and Esther Harding's perspectives." *Quadrant,* 39(1), 17-27.

Schoenl, W. (2014). "Jung's evolving views of Nazi Germany: From 1936 to the end of World War II." *Journal of Analytical Psychology,* 59(2), 245-62.

Schoenl, W., & Peck, D. (2012). "An answer to the question: Was Jung, for a time, a 'Nazi Sympathizer' or Not?" *Jung Journal: Culture & Psyche,* 6(4), 98-105.

Schoenl, W., & Schoenl, L. (2016). "Jung's views of Nazi Germany: The first year and Jung's transition." *Journal of Analytical Psychology,* 61(4), 481-96.

Shapiro, Karl. (1949). "Shapiro to Leonie Adams, 26 July 1949." Virginia Allan Detloff Library, C.G. Jung Institute of San Francisco, CA.

Sherry, J. (2010). *Carl Gustav Jung: Avant-garde conservative.* New York: Palgrave Macmillan.

Sorge, G. (2010). "Psicologia Analitica e Anni Trenta: Il Ruola di C.G. Jung nella 'Internationale Aerztliche Gesellschaft fuer Psychotherapie.'" 1933-1939/40. Doctoral dissertation. University of Zurich, Switzerland.

Sorge, G. (2012). "Jung's presidency of the International General Medical Society of Psychotherapy: New insights." *Jung Journal: Culture & Psyche*, 6(4), 31-53.

Van der Hoop, J.H. (1934a). "Van der Hoop to Jung, 4 March 1934." JA Zurich.

Van der Hoop, J.H . (1934b). "Van der Hoop to Jung, 9 April 1934." JA Zurich.

Wertham, F. (1944, 4 December). "The spirit of Freud. Review of A.A. Brill's *Freud's contribution to psychiatry.*" *The New Republic.* 773-74.

Index

Index

Jaffe, Aniela 2, 70, 74

Japan 34, 39

Jenssen, Christian 3

Jews 4, 9, 10, 11, 26, 33, 49, 51 55, 59, 61

Johns Hopkins University 62

Jung, C.G. v, vi, vii, ix, 1, 2, 3, 4, 5, 6, 7, 8, 9, 10, 11, 12, 13, 14, 15, 16, 17, 19, 20, 21, 22, 23, 24, 25, 26, 27, 28, 29, 30, 31, 32, 33, 34, 35, 37, 38, 39, 40, 41, 42, 43, 44, 45, 46, 47, 48, 49, 50, 51, 52, 53, 54, 55, 56, 57, 58, 59, 60, 61, 62, 63, 64, 65, 67, 68, 69, 70, 71, 72, 73, 74, 75, 76, 77, 78

Jung Archives vi, vii, 8, 56, 67, 68, 70, 76

Jung Biographical Archive vii, 67, 70

Jung Foundation for Analytical Psychology vii, ix, 69

Jung *Gesellschaft* vi, 29

Jung Institute of San Francisco vii, ix, 68, 70, 76, 77

Jungians 55, 58, 64, 76

Kaplan, J. 50, 75

Kirsch, James 16, 52, 71, 75

Knickerbocker, H.R. 30, 53, 63, 72

Kolb, Eugen 49, 50

Kranefeldt, Wolfgang 7, 8, 9, 16, 22, 70, 71, 72

Kretschmer, Ernst 2, 5

Kristallnacht 33

Kuesnacht 2, 4, 31, 33, 44

Lake Constance 45

Lammers, Ann Conrad 2, 6, 10, 71, 75

Laurence, Richard R. vii

Index

Tavistock Clinic vi, 22, 27, 28, 30, 72
Tel Aviv 49
Terry Lectures 29, 30, 54, 59, 62, 63, 72
Third Reich 31, 38

Ullmann, Herman 46
United States vi, vii, 25, 37, 38, 39, 40, 42, 43, 48, 51, 52, 54, 64
University of Geneva 44

van der Hoop, J.H. 13, 14, 15, 19, 34, 71, 78
V-E Day. See Victory in Europe Day
Victory in Europe Day 52, 53, 58, 64
Virginia Allan Detloff Library vii, 68, 70, 76, 77
Visions Seminar 19, 71
von Schnitzler, Baron 17, 49

Wehrmacht 29
Weltwoche 45, 46, 52, 53, 64, 74
Wertham, Fredric 43, 55, 78
West 4, 32, 44, 58
Western Europe 37
Wheelwright Collection vii
Whitney, Elizabeth 58, 68, 70
Wickes, Frances 48
Wolff, Toni 10
World War I 32
World War II v, vi, ix, 16, 35, 37, 39, 42, 46, 48, 50, 51, 57, 64, 77
Wotan 2, 23, 24, 25, 29, 31, 34, 45, 46, 47, 63, 64, 72

About the Authors

William Schoenl is professor emeritus of Modern European history at Michigan State University, where he taught for 45 years. His recent publications include Jung's Evolving Views of Nazi Germany: From 1936 to the End of World War II, *Journal of Analytical Psychology*, 59(2), (April 2014) and An Answer to the Question: Was Jung, for a Time, a "Nazi Sympathizer" or Not?, *Jung Journal*, 6(4), (Fall 2012). His books include *C. G. Jung: His Friendships with Mary Mellon and J. B. Priestley* (Chiron, 1998).

Linda Schoenl, RN, is co-author with William of Jung's Views of Nazi Germany: The First Year and Jung's Transition, *Journal of Analytical Psychology*, 61(4), (September 2016). She was a registered nurse in the Regional Neonatal Intensive Care Unit at Sparrow Health System, Lansing, Michigan for 37 years. She and William were the Nyaka Aids Orphans Foundation Volunteers of the Year (Uganda 2015).

www.ingramcontent.com/pod-product-compliance
Lightning Source LLC
Chambersburg PA
CBHW031447280326
41927CB00037B/379